Out of Bounds

Out of Bounds

Sexual Exploitation in Counselling and Therapy

Janice Russell

SAGE Publications
London • Newbury Park • New Delhi

First published 1993

SAGE Publications Ltd
6 Bonhill Street
London EC2A 4PU

SAGE Publications Inc
2455 Teller Road
Newbury Park, California 91320

SAGE Publications India Pvt Ltd
32, M-Block Market
Greater Kailash – I
New Delhi 110 048

British Library Cataloguing in Publication data

Russell, Janice
  Out of Bounds: Sexual Exploitation in
  Counselling and Therapy
  I. Title
  616.89

  ISBN 0–8039–8533–9
  ISBN 0–8039–8534–7 (pbk)

Library of Congress catalog card number 92–059971

Typeset by Photoprint, Torquay, Devon
Printed in Great Britain by Biddles Ltd, Guildford, Surrey

CONTENTS

ACKNOWLEDGEMENTS

This book has developed from four years' work and has been very much an ongoing process rather than a one-off task. I am therefore indebted to many people who have aided this process over that time. To get the whole thing started, I am grateful to Brian Gibbons for having faith in my ability and for his encouragement and support in many ways.

My great thanks to the people who contributed directly by having the courage to share their own experiences with me. My greatest fear has been that in reading about themselves they would feel exploited yet again, and I hope that I have done justice to their stories.

I also appreciate the informal discussions with colleagues and with participants on workshops who have helped me to try out ideas and challenged me with their insights.

Most of the research for the work was unfunded and depended on scrimping and saving. One much appreciated exception was a donation from the Alec van Berchem Charitable Trust.

My appreciation goes to Val Hill for supporting the book proposal. For help with the manuscript, thanks to Tim Bond for a useful reading and suggestions, to Lynn Sheppard for almost reading Chapter 1, and then giving her indubitable brand of incisive feedback on Chapter 8, and to Graham Dexter for reading the manuscript in every stage, for giving me thuggish feedback at times, for teaching me to format, and for many a stimulating discussion.

Many people have supported me in a personal sense, too numerous to be named. Special mention must be made to my parents Joyce and Jack for their unfailing backing and love, to my children Kezzie and Sam for accepting me as a working mum and for being smashing, and to Dexy for his love, understanding and humour. All my other friends will know who they are and that their encouragement is valued highly, whether through discussion or by keeping a hand near the teapot on a bad day.

INTRODUCTION

The aim of this book is to introduce and explore the issue of sexual exploitation in counselling and therapy. It has two main objectives within this. The first is to inform the practitioner and the interested reader about what sexual exploitation within this context is and how it might occur. The second is to look at how the professions involved might begin to consider the subject and to introduce strategies to deal with and prevent such exploitation as far as possible.

The book is inspired by and informed by the experiences of people who, in the client seat, experienced what they saw as sexual exploitation within their counselling or therapy relationships. Research was carried out over a four year period, during which I interviewed about forty people who felt that they had been exploited. During this time I also had a myriad of informal discussions with people who were interested in the issues, from either the client or the counsellor point of view. The structure of the research has been fairly loose, then, and is of a qualitative rather than a quantitative nature. All unreferenced quotations and epigraphs are attributable, to the research participants.

Over the four years, I also collected what I could from other research findings, and was stimulated by my sociology background to explore the issues from a wider perspective. My own experience as a counsellor, supervisor and trainer within counselling, and specifically of working with sexual abuse, also informs the approach to, and outcome of, the work.

The book is divided into two parts. The first draws on desk-based and action research to inform the reader around the subject. Chapter 1 gives an overview and conceptualisation of the problem and locates it professionally and historically. Chapter 2 looks at the effects of sexual exploitation on the client, and draws on available research from the United States and on original research in Britain. Chapter 3 summarises some of the original research to give a flavour of the process of exploitation and how and where it may occur within the therapeutic process. Chapter 4 looks at the practitioner.

Chapters 5 and 6 look at how sexuality and power may be conceptualised, and how these are relevant within the therapeutic process and within exploitative practice. They attempt to integrate theory with the practical base of the research findings.

The second part of the book focuses on the implications of the work for practice. Chapter 7 looks at some of the ethical dimensions to the problem under review, at codes of ethics and their limitations, and makes some suggestion as to what needs to be made clearer in such codes. Chapter 8 begins to explore how the practitioner might be alert to the possibilities of sexual exploitation within the therapeutic relationship, and offers perspectives on how this might be addressed within supervision and training. Chapter 9 offers some concluding comments and recommendations where further work needs to be done.

A cautionary rider is made that this is not an exhaustive text, and not to be read as a 'what the problem is and how to solve it' manual. Rather, it is an attempt to introduce and conceptualise a current problem within the therapeutic professions, to juxtapose it against ethical desirability, and to begin to consider it in greater depth. The book is offered in a spirit of inquiry and it is hoped that at the very least it will stimulate discussion, thought and further exploration, with the aim of enhancing client service.

PART ONE ASPECTS OF THE PROBLEM OF EXPLOITATIVE PRACTICE

1

CONTEXTS AND CONCEPTS OF SEXUAL EXPLOITATION

> I can't say that it was lust, I can't say that it was fetish, I can't say that it was therapy.

In the 1980s, we saw an explosion of media attention to the problems of sexual abuse and exploitation. Newspapers, television, books and helplines all gave the subject much attention, to the point where many people would contend that the subject of sexual abuse is now less of a taboo than ever before. Moreover, there is increasing recognition that people from all backgrounds and professions may be the perpetrators of abuse or exploitative practice.

In response, we now have a philosophy of how to help the sexually abused. A central strategy for such help is the use of psychotherapy, a term used in its widest sense. It is, then, all the more disturbing to realise that clients may be sexually exploited within the therapeutic relationship, a realisation that is becoming reluctantly conceded by professional groups.

One of the aims of this work is to add to the body of knowledge on the subject in the hope that it will help to raise awareness about sexually exploitative practice within therapeutic relationships. The orientation is towards preventive as well as reparative practice.

Two major myths need to be dispelled. One is that *our* professionals do not abuse. It is my guess that this myth is as prevalent within the profession as outside it – one of the reactions I have had to my research on the subject is along the lines of 'yes, I know it happens in the States, but surely not here'. There needs to be overt admission that this is a problem for *all* the therapeutic professions, whatever the theoretical model, and whether or not they are statutory or voluntary bodies.

The second myth is that we do actually talk about abuse more than we ever did, and that we now understand what it means. This is mythical because although we use the words repeatedly, I am not convinced that there is a shared meaning attached to them, either for the abused or for the interested listener. In other words, sexual abuse has become a blanket term which in fact can refer to a myriad of experiences and behaviours.

I must also stress that I am using the terms sexual abuse and sexual exploitation interchangeably for conceptual ease. I use them to mean behaviour or experience where one person in a position of trust, or with a position of power over another, abuses this position, without the informed consent of the other party, for their own sexual gratification. This concept reflects my own view and does not necessarily reflect the views of all the participants. It is a working definition which is intended to be enabling rather than to act as a constraint.

The work as a whole, then, will show that in the field of therapy, as in any other walk of life, professionals do abuse. It will also look more closely at what exploitative practice in therapy actually means, drawing on the diversity of experience of clients involved.

This book depends heavily on research and on the experience of those clients, and on therapists all over Britain, who have been involved in it over the last four years. I will refer throughout to those experiences and will quote from participants, where appropriate, in an effort to impart some sense of how they see the problem and how it has affected them. Any (mis)interpretations are mine alone.

This will be augmented by the research available from the United States, and on historical documentation. This first chapter, then, will try to provide a context and an introduction to the problem under review.

Providing a context

> He was a CPN [Community Psychiatric Nurse] then, I didn't know what kind of therapy this was, I didn't even know he was a CPN, he called himself a therapist. They all did . . . I didn't even know what a CPN was until later on . . . I don't know what kind of therapy he was doing, he never told me. I now know that he was doing psychotherapy which he was not trained to do.

The above quote from one of the participants in this work is not entirely untypical. It seems that many workers within the field of mental health work are assumed, either by themselves, their clients, or their organisations, to have some therapeutic skills. In professional circles there has been much debate on what might constitute the differences between counselling and psychotherapy, and there are a wide variety of practices which may fall under either heading.[1] I am also aware from my practice experience as a trainer and researcher that many workers who have received little or no training in the area are now expected to have a counselling dimension to their job, for example health advisers.

The term therapist, then, needs some clarification. In this work, I am using it in a broad sense to mean any worker who engages in a relationship with a client where the stated aims are to help that client alleviate psychological distress or to enhance self-understanding, with a view to changing something in the client's life. The therapeutic relationship in this sense is seen as either a precondition or a tool of the helping process. The process essentially revolves around the idea of the *talking cure*, whether or not that is augmented by alternative forms of communication, for example visual or tactile.

Therapy, then, in this broad sense of a one-to-one talking cure, is not a new practice. Historical and sociological analysis suggest that it has developed alongside the discipline of psychology from magical, religious and medicinal discourse (see for example: Thomas, 1971; Foucault, 1977; Rose, 1990). It is difficult to identify a precise moment of inception, but it struck me during my research that we might take the practice of mesmerism as one of the earliest examples of psychotherapy.

The task of mesmerism was to explore the mind of the patient in order to resolve distress, thus giving early recognition to the concept of mental health. The method involved a one to one talking cure, the relationship between practitioner and patient served as the tool for the job, and the practitioner claimed some professional status. Without claiming to be definitive, then, this seems an appropriate starting point. Moreover, mesmeric practice was the focus over two hundred years ago for some of the tensions and conflicts pertinent to this work, i.e. the question of the sexual dynamic within the therapeutic relationship.

More specifically, the practice of mesmerism provides us with an historical precedent to the consideration of the ethics of sexual contact between therapists and patients. The work of Mesmer and his followers had led to an acknowledgement of the possibility of erotic feelings being aroused within the therapeutic relationship, and to concern about the possibilities of exploitative practice. I was interested to discover that Louis XVI was so concerned about the etiquette and the ethics of this therapeutic practice that he appointed a team of commissioners to conduct an investigation. The outcome of this investigation was known as 'Bailly's Secret Report', and it highlighted some of the major areas of concern.

One important aspect was the very acknowledgement of the possibilities of erotic interaction between the parties:

> The woman is always magnetized by the man . . . whatever the nature of the illness, it does not divest us of our own sex, nor does it entirely remove us from the power of the other sex . . . It is not surprising that the senses are inflamed. (Chertok and de Saussure, 1979: 10–11)

This acknowledgement was supported by an understanding of the influential nature of the relationship: 'All the greatest abuses . . . may follow from this influence which you acquire over your patients' (ibid., 1979: 14).

It would seem that this combination of sexuality and influence was taken very seriously. One practitioner, Deleuze, having acknowledged the 'erotic complications' of the 'magnetic' relationship had gone as far as to recommend the avoidance of certain situations. Young women being treated by young or middle-aged men were not seen without a chaperone, and indeed many magnetists worked with a third party present (ibid., 1979: 18).

We may note that this was as much for the protection of the magnetist as of the patient, for Bailly's report had concluded that patients showed a 'relatively complaisant attitude in this respect' (ibid., 1979: 17), that is in entering into sexual relations with their magnetists.

Already then we see certain themes being recognised within the therapeutic relationship of mesmerism – erotic feelings, power, influence, complaisance, vulnerabilities. We may note also a heterosexist bias to the analysis which is indicative of its time, particularly in the sense that practitioners would be male, and often the clients female.

This bias is not exclusive to the ethos of the time, however, and we still see heterosexist bias and assumptions being made in the practice and theory of therapy. One of my concerns is to illustrate that exploitative practice is not confined to male therapists and female clients, which some of the few major works in this area would contend.[2] In terms of practice, one of the most extreme examples of heterosexist exploitation that I know of was where a therapist offered his client's lesbianism as justification for his entering into a sexual relationship with her – her sexual orientation was seen as the problem, his exploitation the cure. We need then to locate our understanding of this problem within a challenging exploration of the context in which we operate.

We are indebted to Freud for the next major acknowledgement of the sexual dynamic. Within his conceptualisation of transference, he recognised the power of the erotic component: '. . . the patient's falling in love is induced by the analytic situation and is not to be attributed to the charms of his own person' (in Chertok and de Saussure, 1979: 145). For whatever criticisms may be made of Freud's own biases or blind spots, this gives important recognition that certain feelings or experience will be more to do with the *conditions* of the relationship than with the individuals concerned, and will at the very least be influenced by these. This is central to the practitioner's understanding and therefore to the client's.

Interestingly, however, despite conceptualising its corollary, countertransference, he seems to have had little to say on the therapist falling in love with or being attracted to the patient. This is a crucial area to be addressed, from whichever theoretical perspective.

As we trace the development of therapeutic practice, we can see how sexuality entered the arena from another perspective, that is, as the site of treatment. Charcot, for example, had used sexual feelings and experience as part of the therapeutic technique. In the notorious Salpatriere, female patients were stimulated in their 'hysterogenic zones', allegedly demonstrating 'sexual responses which sometimes reached a state of orgasm'. Such techniques were often used publicly, and Freud apparently witnessed many such demonstrations (Chertok and de Saussure, 1979: 88).

There are, of course, several accounts of eminent therapists having sexual encounters with their clients from the beginning of this century onwards. Freud's own disciple Ferenczi is often cited in this bracket, and recent works would suggest that this occurred within a context of many blurred boundaries grounded in a theoretical approach of 'reciprocity' (Stanton, 1990). Wilhelm Reich saw satisfactory sexual release as a 'prime goal of therapy', and went on to marry a patient (Marmor, 1972: 3). Jung is said to have seduced one of his first analytic patients (Herman et al., 1987). The problem under review is not new.

Some psychotherapists advocated sexual relationships with their patients as a therapeutic tool, for example Dr James McCartney, who was subsequently expelled from the American Psychiatry Association (Lange and Hirsh, 1981). Sex therapy, of course, was developed as a 'discipline' during the 1960s, and is still practised to deal with 'sexual dysfunction'. This concept essentialises sexual behaviour to specific functions and renders measurable such states

as desire, arousal and orgasm (Cooper, 1988). Within this, surro-
gate therapy, first used by Masters and Johnson (1970), is still
advocated by some practitioners, though its application is now more
constrained than at one time by legal, ethical and practical considerations (Cole and Dryden, 1988). Indeed, sex therapy is now treated
with much more caution as the thin line between therapy and
exploitation is recognised. Martin Cole contends that this can make
for less efficient therapy (Cole and Dryden, 1988).

The trend for advocating sex as a therapeutic technique seems to
be declining on both sides of the Atlantic, but leaves a legacy of
some blurred areas. The blurs are not exclusive to this school, and
many of the humanistic growth type therapies leave unclear boundaries too, either within the theory or within the models of practice
demonstrated by their advocates.

Fritz Perls, for example, did not so much advocate the exercise of
sexual activity as a therapy in a formal sense as fail to rule it out. If
biography and autobiography are to be believed, he seemed to find
it essential to allow of any 'real encounter' in both his personal and
professional life, and to have enjoyed sex with virtually anyone who
would have him, either in or out of the therapeutic relationship
(Shepard, 1976).

While the problem of sexual relations within the therapeutic
arena are not a new consideration, then, it would seem that they
have rarely been considered from the point of view of the client.
The problem has been unnamed – we acknowledge the theoretical
possibilities and the practices of some of the better known mentors.
In the United States, considerable research has gone into interviewing practitioners. Research with clients as subject seems consider-
ably rarer.

Current practice – conceptualising the sexually exploitative

The precedents for sexual encounter within the therapeutic relationship which have been cited so far are either condoned or con-
demned by the profession. This leads us to consider that if, in
condemnation, there is recognition of *inappropriate* sexual behaviour, we must, over time, have developed some notion of *appropriate* boundaries of sexual behaviour.

This is reflected in the development of codes of practice and
ethics which has accompanied the professionalisation of the thera-

peutic enterprise. Indeed, the very fact of having a written code of behaviour is itself reflective of an interesting process of regulation.

Paul Rock suggests that if there have to be statute laws, then the social rules have lost their potency – thus laws acquire a certain quality of contrivance (1973: 122–97). In a sense, they presuppose some heterodoxy of moral perspective, that is recognising that there will be differing codes and standards, thus their own weakness is tacitly recognised in their very creation. Within the therapeutic professions, then, this would suggest that the ethical codes which consider the norms of appropriate behaviour recognise the possibility of their transgression.

It will be helpful here to consider what these norms are. For example, my own governing body, the British Association for Counselling (BAC), has recently revised its codes of ethics and practice. It now states in the ethical code that: 'Counselling is a non-exploitative activity. Its basic values are integrity, impartiality, and respect' (BAC *Code of Ethics and Practice*, 1990: A.1.).

This then is seen as a principle, which is applied more specifically within the code of practice to the counselling situation: 'Counsellors must not exploit their clients financially, sexually, emotionally, or in any other way' (ibid.: 2.2.6.).

The prohibition is set within a context, namely that the code can offer only a framework which will not resolve all ethical and practical issues, but might offer the optimum chance of doing so. This seems to me to be a realistic guideline, all the more so because it recognises its limitations. I also like the fact that exploitation is seen as the issue, and that sexual exploitation is one form of this.

The BAC code is fairly typical, and details of others may be found in Chapter 3. Where they fail, however, is in clarifying what is meant by sexual or sexually exploitative. This is no criticism, rather the seizing of an opportunity to introduce a problematic which for me is central to the consideration of this subject, namely what constitutes the sexual, and what makes for the exploitative?

I have been struck by two reactions which I have encountered throughout the four years in which I have been researching this area. The first, from both professionals and non-professionals, is an assumption that the problem under consideration is one of genital contact within the consulting room. The second, from people who feel that they have been exploited, is a doubting of their own experience if it did not involve such behaviour.

Research conducted elsewhere, notably the United States, has shed some light on the notion of appropriateness. Gartrell et al. (1986), and Kardener et al. (1973), use sexual contact to refer to contact which is intended to 'arouse or satisfy sexual desire' in either

therapist or client. Adams talks about 'pressured sexual situations
. . . in which someone in a subservient position is used for another's
gratification, profit or lust' (1987: 61).

Rapp, in his discussion of 'sexual misconduct', makes a more
forceful definition: 'an abuse of power to obtain sexual gratification
that one would not otherwise obtain' (1987: 193), and likens it to
rape in which 'consent of a sort is obtained by false pretences'
(ibid.). We see here a movement in the concept from the evocation
of sexual feeling, to a recognition of a power dynamic within the
therapeutic relationship which is open to exploitation for the
gratification of the therapist. Rapp's definition also recognises the
importance of the concept of informed consent, and in his use of the
notion of false pretences, implicitly recognises the complexities of
this concept.

Coleman and Schaefer (1986) also recognise the complexities,
and offer one of the most explicit expositions of what might
constitute abuse. They use a continuum model, continuum in the
sense of a linear progression with polarised extremes to categorise
'psychological, covert and overt abuse'. Covert abuse includes
'sexual hugs', 'professional voyeurism', and 'sexual gazes'; overt
abuse ranges from 'sexualizing remarks' to 'sexual intercourse';
while psychological abuse represents a tackling of the emotional
needs of the counsellor rather than of the client (ibid.: 342–3).

In terms of what may make a whole range of behaviours
exploitative, Smith (1988) makes the following observation:

> Intentionality and awareness of consequences, as well as the setting of
> limits for nonsexual relations must be a part of this picture. . . . Thus a
> friendly, supportive pat on the shoulder during a time of grief, for
> example, does not constitute sexual intimacy. (1988: 60)

These points offer some useful indicators and insights into the
complexities of the problematic. We may then extrapolate that a
working understanding of appropriate behaviour will be behaviour
where:

- The therapist sets and takes responsibility for clear boundaries
  with the client.
- The therapist does not exploit the client either covertly or
  overtly for his or her own gratification.
- The client's psychological needs are seen as the dominant focus
  of the relationship.
- The therapist has an awareness and an understanding of the
  intentionality of his or her own interventions, an understanding
  which is communicated to the client.

- The therapist has a clear understanding of the consequences of those interventions.

The difficulty still remains however that these insights remain prescriptive without exploration of the interpretative nature of interactions. Intentionality is not enough if we are not skilled enough to check out whether this is conveyed to and understood by the client. We also need to check constantly that we are understanding how the client perceives the situation. There is some evidence from my research and from my own experience as a trainer and supervisor that basic listening and responding skills, which help to clarify communication, are all too often overlooked or omitted by experienced practitioners.

Further, we return to the question of what constitutes the sexual, whether in sexual gaze, sexual hug, or sexual act. Part of the method and the purpose of this work is to expand awareness of the client's perspective, and to demonstrate the range of interpretations of behaviour, regardless of the conscious intentionality of the therapist.

My own perspective is that there is a whole range of possible consequences of any intervention. I would contend that even a hug during a time of grief may, in vulnerability, be perceived as a precursor for intimate contact. This is not to prescribe no physical contact, but rather to widen the possibilities for our own awareness and thus, ultimately, to ensure the most ethical and effective service for the client.

Naming the problem

Having looked at historical precedence and at some notion of what might be deemed role-appropriate, how do we know that there is a problem now? In the process of conducting this research, and in response to people questioning why I was doing it, I found myself rejoining that my awareness was stimulated in Sussex in 1988. At that time I was involved with a group of women on a mental health subcommittee. This group was approached by two women who were complaining of inappropriate sexual behaviour from their therapists. Various initiatives came from different quarters, notably from the women themselves, and my response was to start researching. I linked into this immediately from experience and interest in sexual abuse. I had also recognised that there would be some connection here between specific instances of exploitation and attitudes of sexism and heterosexism which I had noticed within the therapeutic profession.

As I made this response, I was stimulated to recall other levels and times of awareness. I remembered a woman who was my client several years ago who had suffered consistent and repeated sexual assault within her family. She told me of her deep distrust of a worker at one of the (then) recently set up helplines, and her sense that some of his verbal responses and his manner had felt abusive. I was intrigued, trusting that her experience was valid and wondering whether her reception of his interventions belied an intentionality or not.

Other memories crept in. I remembered accounts by friends who had gone to a particular therapist for help with sexual difficulties, and whose feelings had ranged from vulnerability to outrage and humiliation at being put through a programme of sex therapy which included masturbation on the couch. 'Why did you do it if you didn't want to', I asked, and they had answered that they thought he knew what he was doing, that they wanted to be helped and so would try anything. I remembered another memory of a friend disclosing to me that she had been in a sexual relationship with a man whom she had met through telephone counselling. He suggested they meet, and the sexual relationship developed.

With hindsight and experience, I wonder how many other people know of and recognise similar incidents. My sense is that the phenomenon is something like Betty Friedan's 'problem with no name', the bored housewife syndrome, that made such a powerful impact on women in the early 1960s (1965). Certainly since I have been researching, I have met many people who know of 'someone to whom it has happened'. So perhaps it is not so much a question of how do we know there is a problem, as recognising that through the efforts of user groups and interested professionals, within which there will be some overlap, the problem of exploitative sexual behaviour within the therapeutic relationship is now being named. It is certainly only within the last year or two that the professions have begun to overtly acknowledge and address the problem.[3]

So what is it, this problem? As far as I am aware, there is little research in Britain on the subject, although some user groups are at present collecting and collating information.[4] My limited findings lead me to conclude that there are clients who have felt abused by their therapists through a whole range of interventions and behaviours. These have included episodes of kissing and stroking; lengthy affairs; inappropriate and offensive responses, demeanour and verbal utterances; inappropriate dress; refusal to acknowledge erotic components of the relationship; ambiguous hugs; one-off sexual intercourse; fellatio with the therapist; and intimate physical touch as part of the 'diagnostic procedure'. The common and bottom line is that in all these instances, the client has felt that the therapist has overstepped the boundaries. This seems to me to be the most useful way of conceptualising if we are then to find ways of reparative and preventive work.

Clarity and contracting are two key issues here, two themes which will be returned to in Chapter 9 on recommendations. Clarity, because this seems to me to be the best method of checking out that we as counsellors understand precisely what the client is telling us, and, conversely, that they understand what we are telling them. Contracting is the essential foundation of high quality therapeutic practice. We know that we need to contract boundaries of time, space and purpose. It seems appropriate that we should at this point contract the boundaries of the relationship, to state overtly that it will not be a relationship of friendship, love or sexual encounter.

For some of the clients referred to in this work, it seems that the failure to make an overt statement might have reinforced their unwitting complaisance in behaviour is the belief that it was therapeutic. One participant in this research allowed her therapist to touch the inside of her thighs. She experienced great discomfort with this both at the time and afterwards, yet had reluctantly allowed it as she felt 'in a therapeutic state'. Others experienced a niggle at the time but chose not to challenge behaviour as it occurred in the belief that the therapist knew better than them, and that the behaviour had some value. Perhaps a clearer contract would help clients to know what *not* to expect, and thus help them to trust their own misgivings.

As it is, many of the participants in this research found their interpretation and perception changed over time. This seems to be partly due to the ambivalent responses which they experienced, and the lack of clear contracting seems to have exacerbated the guilt which they experienced over this. They felt it was wrong, but had no clear guidelines from the therapist to reinforce this. This may seem self-evident, but seems to me to be an important point. To accept this is not to understate or diminish plausibility, merely to recognise that it often takes time to make any kind of sense of our experiences.

When individuals feel hurt and betrayed, the task may become more difficult. Often they feel unable to tell anyone, as a sense of guilt or shame may ensue. The next chapter will detail some of the processes and effects of exploitative practice. The point for this section is that part of the problem we are looking at is that exploitative practice may not be recognised as problematic immediately, or may be internally recognised yet unarticulated.

Other scenarios

The problem is not confined to the therapist–client scenario. Another area of potential for inappropriate sexual conduct is that between tutor/trainer and student. Some of the participants in my research felt that they had been exploited by trainers or tutors, or else had been involved in courses where a sexual relationship had taken place between a tutor and another student. In all cases, this had led to either feelings of abuse or of extreme discomfort, with group dynamics being affected in a way which was felt to be detrimental because of its secret and illicit nature.

In this situation, there is again a power differential which needs to be borne in mind. A salutary lesson for me occurred in a recent workshop, which may serve as a good illustration of the kind of dynamics involved. I was running a workshop on the very theme of sexuality in the counselling relationship and, due to misunderstandings, arrived twenty minutes late. As a co-tutor had started up the introductions, I omitted to make a group contract, for the first time in many years. The workshop was experiential, and in the tea break one of the participants approached me in some distress to ask if it was acceptable to opt out. The workshop had provoked some issues for her which she found difficult, and while acknowledging that she would like to work with those in her own way, she felt she needed my permission not to at that time. The issues concerned were not between her and me, but nevertheless reminded me sharply of the perceived authority of the tutor. We must all have had the experience of following an exercise despite discomfort in the hope that it will prove a learning experience, but again it must be clearly contracted that we do not have to do what is suggested.

Yet another dimension to the problem is illustrated by therapists who know of other therapists who are alleged to be exploiting their clients sexually. This was exemplified sharply by the experience of one participant who had such a disclosure from a client, in confidence, who was himself a therapist. This was mirrored by less extreme experiences of others who either suspected colleagues, or who had clients who reported abuse. The issues here are the conflict between confidentiality and the well-being of clients. The feeling of discomfort with possible collusion was well illustrated by one social worker who worked with a psychiatrist who she felt was behaving unethically: 'I felt like a Nazi, colluding with something which I knew to be wrong yet could do nothing about.'

So, naming the problem reminds us of how complex it is. This work makes no attempt to estimate its size, and the research undertaken here does not claim to be either exhaustively representative or a counting exercise. It is, rather, an attempt to identify the nature of the beast in all its complexities and acknowledge its ambiguities. My hope is that through listening to client's experiences, we as therapists can sensitise and educate ourselves, and ultimately do what we can to ensure the best and safest possible experience for clients, in a context of open discussion and support for ourselves.

Values

Having tried to contextualise the problem historically, ethically and conceptually, the final objective of this chapter is to try to contextualise it within a system of values within the counselling world. All mental health workers fulfil a particular function in society. Their role is inexorably bound up with the discourse of psychology emergent over the last two centuries, with its focus on the rehabilitation of the individual. Within this, their practice, however liberal or client-centred, is fundamentally linked to concepts of normality and deviance.

Further, as has been argued extensively by philosophers and by the anti-psychiatry movement (see for example, Szasz, 1971; Foucault, 1985), this function may be seen as extending way beyond the confines of the specific therapeutic relationship to a wider network of social control. Not only do therapists have a say in what constitutes normality and deviance, the practice of therapy is now widely recognised as having a central contribution to make in the field of social discipline. As Foucault puts it:

> The question is no longer simply 'Has the act been established . . . what law punishes this offence?', but 'What would be the most appropriate measures to take: How do we see the future development of the offender? What would be the best way of rehabilitating him?' (1985: 19)

For Foucault, the humanitarian language of the mental health professions is coexistent with a governance which is characterised by surveillance and tooled by confession. In other words, our behaviour is not only observed through psychological media (such as, intelligence tests, school reports, medical records, therapeutic consultations), but also then assessed, recorded, and used as a method of social policing.

Despite the increasing philosophical and sociological analyses of deviance, treatment and social control, which have had at least some impact on the social work profession generally (see for example, Hart, 1979), the counselling and therapeutic professions have in common a tendency to see themselves as only providing a helping relationship, and a traditional reluctance to acknowledge how value-laden their disciplines are. Where this is attempted, it seems it is represented as a polar opposite, that is to say, as being *only* a means of social control (see for example, Masson, 1988).

The reality is more complex. Consider the following examples of discussions of counselling and psychotherapy. Nelson-Jones (1982) defines counselling as having two distinct facets: it may be a helping relationship, which involves stipulating some 'central counsellor qualities', or 'core conditions' such as empathy, respect, congruence and genuineness; or it may be a set of activities or methods, which may represent theoretical viewpoints. Munro et al. (1983) use 'counselling' to cover the various skills and principles of helping, and regard it as a problem-solving activity. Here the different methods constitute counselling when 'certain other conditions of the relationship are met', these being of an ethical nature – confidentiality, and the emphasis on the personal responsibility of the client for their own behaviour (Munro et al., 1983: 11–14). Rogers and Stevens (1967: 13–28) see psychotherapy as a helping relationship, and suggest that 'the therapist needs to be psychologically mature to facilitate it'. Graham Cooper (1988: 2) suggests that counselling should help the client to be 'able to see her difficulties more objectively'.

As a counsellor myself, I have no difficulty in accepting the spirit of these conceptualisations. Nevertheless, it is worth noting that they suggest some kind of value-free individualistic process whereby the counsellor helps in an ethically commendable, empathic yet objective fashion. Yet what constitutes ethics, psychological maturity, objective, genuineness, congruence? They may all be broken down and defined, yet all relate to values.

This does not have to be a 'bad thing' – rather it feels important to acknowledge this openly, whereas my sense is that the profession has distanced itself from overt connection to its philosophical principles, and, at worst, is trapped in 'sorry illusion' that it may be 'conducted in a totally value-free atmosphere' (Barnhouse, 1978: 536). In reality, it operates in a social and political arena – values again. This is perhaps most easily recognised by the creation of feminist and black counselling bodies which recognise that differing values operate – presumably one of the reasons for separate organisation (and it is my guess that the reasons are complex) is that the mainstream networks were not perceived as operating the relevant value system.

Many definitions and conceptions of counselling are at pains to use the notion of unconditional positive regard as a means of ensuring that counselling is carried out within the value system of clients. Yet this is not strictly true; we all have our limits in this respect. For example, a counsellor may be prepared to suspend judgement in helping a rapist believing that this is a means to a valued outcome, namely the cessation of the activity. However, if that rapist declared a desire to be better able to continue the activity without getting caught the counsellor may well feel unable to continue the work and may cease to offer confidentiality at this stage. Indeed if the counsellor did not, then it is my guess that he or she would be seen to be behaving both unprofessionally and unethically.

If the whole practice of counselling incorporates values and value systems, then it should be no surprise that it also incorporates some specific sexual values, both in its theory and its practice. More will be said on this in Chapter 5. The point here is that however successful we are in suspending values and judgements, there is always some value-laden influence upon us, whether in the theoretical or practical perspective from which we operate, or in the ethical code to which we subscribe. Our values, then, must be overtly recognised for best practice to ensue, and clients must know these in making their choice of counsellor.

Summary

This chapter has outlined that there is a problem within the therapeutic professions of sexual exploitation of clients. Therapeutic professions are used to include all those involved with the mental health of people from a perspective which offers a talking cure. So far, little research has been done on the subject in Britain, although precedence is known historically and elsewhere.

The term sexual exploitation is seen as complex, and one of the aims of this book is to tease out what behaviour may be included in this term, and in what situations. It is recognised that the client's perspective will be crucial to arriving at a deeper understanding. It is recognised also that the problem area may include relationships between trainers and students. It is suggested as well that many practitioners will have come into contact with this problem in some form or another.

The notion of sexual exploitation leads us to remember that the therapeutic professions will have some notion of appropriate behaviour, and that this leads us to best conceptualise the problem in terms of boundaries. Finally, we recognise that the theory and practice of therapy is itself value based, and that there is a need to be overt about this.

Food for thought

1. In reading through this chapter, do any memories occur for you of people affected in some way through inappropriate sexual behaviour? What thoughts and feelings are provoked for you?
2. Have you ever been aware of feeling sexually attracted to or flirtatious with your own clients, or of a professional therapist being attracted to you? What are the thoughts and feelings that accompany such awareness?

Notes

1   The BAC revised *Code of Ethics and Practice* (1990: 3.3), for example, suggests that:

> It is not possible to make a generally accepted distinction between counselling and psychotherapy. There are well founded traditions which use the terms interchangeably and others which distinguish them. Regardless of the theoretical approaches preferred by individual counsellors, there are ethical issues which are common to all counselling situations.

2   Peter Rutter (1990), for example, in his book *Sex in the Forbidden Zone* makes his whole argument from a Jungian perspective within a patriarchal model.
3   The British Association for Counselling, for example, has started addressing a number of complaints. The British Psychological Society addressed the theme of exploitation at its 1992 conference.
4   See for example the user networks detailed in Chapter 9.

2

EFFECTS ON CLIENTS

> I suppose because of my history and because of what I am trying to work through, there is that fear in me that I make myself a victim and have I made myself a victim again. I find that very hard to forgive in him, because he was the one person who should have helped me with that. I don't see that I made myself a victim, I don't think there was any way in which I did that, but it's taken me a year of battling to believe that.

It is my belief that many therapists will have some knowledge of the effects of a sexually exploitative relationship on their clients, either consciously or otherwise. I say this because many clients will have experience of abusive relationships, either overt or covert. Moreover, the available research suggests that more than one half of practising therapists will work with a client who has experienced sexual intimacy/exploitation with a previous therapist (Pope and Bouhoutsos, 1986).

The effects of any abusive relationship seem to fall into various categories – impaired ability to trust, experiencing a threat to security and an interruption to the continuity of self-image, depressive feelings, guilt, anger, despair. All these and more are well represented within this particular form of abuse.

Moreover, it must be acknowledged that there may be a feeling of double betrayal in the sense that the client has placed trust in someone who would not only be *expected* to be responsible and caring, but also who has claimed the specific ability to help the client heal former hurts, or to learn to live his or her life with more fulfilment. The therapist is thus invested with particular responsibilities by both parties, and occupies a unique role in the client's life. Betrayal provokes an intensity of deep feelings.

In my own research, there seemed to be quite a high proportion of participants who were working on resolving previous sexual abuse when they were then exploited by the therapist. This perception is echoed in the American research findings. In this case, there is the tendency for exploitation to consolidate, or lock in, some of those feelings which the clients may have carried around, unresolved, for years. This seems particularly damaging as it reinforces the clients' (faulty) message to themselves that exploitation is something they at very least deserve, and probably ask for or invite.

Such feelings manifest in different ways, ranging from immediate anger to desperation and suicidal feelings, with a whole host of possibilities in between. To shed further light here, it might be helpful to look at some of the effects already documented in research from the United States, and then to explore in greater detail those outlined by participants in my own research. In this way, readers will be able to familiarise themselves with how such exploitation may damage the client. Practitioners may then be in a better position to help, and clients may be better able to understand that such abuse is not their fault or responsibility. I may add that there is of course an overlap between the two groups.

Understanding how better to help or to recover will necessitate comprehension of what specific problems may arise within the subsequent therapy. Deeper understanding will also hopefully reinforce the ethical prohibition on therapist–client sex.

The American experience

In the United States, several states have introduced legislation to support the prohibition of therapist–client sexual contact. Kenneth Pope (1989) suggests that this reflects acknowledgement of the serious harm which may be incurred in this situation. So far, all the available research suggests that this is the case. Pope cites Durre's (1980) review of the literature which concludes that: 'amatory and sexual interaction between client and therapist . . . is detrimental if not devastating to the client' (Durre, 1980: 243, quoted in Pope, 1989: 40).

Pope's experience and familiarity with this area of research has led him to formulate a clinical syndrome – therapist–patient sex syndrome – which is associated with therapist–client sexual contact. This comprises at least ten 'major damaging aspects' for the client, which are:

1   Ambivalence in the client's feelings towards the therapist, and in whether or not this should be disclosed; this may include investing the therapist with a parental or even Godlike authority.
2   Guilt, the mistaken feeling that this was somehow the client's fault.
3   Emptiness and isolation.
4   Sexual confusion, in that the therapist might have sexualised

issues that were originally non-sexual, for example, responding to the need for physical comfort with a sexual intervention.

5 Impaired ability to trust, as once trust has been betrayed the client will be fearful of investing it again.
6 Identity and role reversal, in that the client may feel responsible for the therapist's feelings and actions, and become the therapist's therapist.
7 Emotional lability or dyscontrol, the tendency to feel strong and varied emotions in inappropriate (that is, unsupportive) situations.
8 Suppressed rage.
9 Increased suicide risk.
10 Cognitive dysfunction, for example the inability to concentrate, preoccupation with what has happened, flashbacks etc. (Pope, 1989: 40–5).

Sonne et al. (1985) have conceptualised the effects in different but complementary terms. In working with a group of women, they found that three major clinical issues emerged repeatedly, which were poor ability to trust, poor self-concept, and difficulties in expressing anger. They suggest that low investment in trust applies to the self as well as to others, in that clients would question their own perception and judgement in previous and present relationships and in their own actions (ibid.: 184). The thinking here is along the lines of 'why didn't I see this coming?', 'how did I contribute?', etc. Such mistrust can contribute to the sense of isolation acknowledged by Pope (1989).

Poor self-concept is seen as having four aspects which manifested as low self-esteem, dependency, desire for specialness, and sexuality. Feelings of degradation, worthlessness and powerlessness were common for the women worked with, as was a fear of being alone and independent despite a demonstrated ability for and pleasure in independence prior to the event. Desire for specialness relates to the loss of a relationship in which the client felt uniquely special to the therapist, whereas problems with sexuality might arise from the feeling of sexuality becoming the site of blame, for instance, 'my sexual feelings and behaviour have got me into this mess'.

These findings are consistent with those in my own research, although I would stress that not all people will show every symptom, and that neither is the list exhaustive. They are also consistent with known effects of sexual abuse in wider scenarios. They certainly fit into my own model of working with sexual abuse which conceptualises such experience as involving massive invisible loss and a mixed grieving experience. For example, it is not uncommon for someone abused by a trusted person (such as a parent or a friend), to feel tremendous ambivalence as they experience opposing feelings of affection and rage. Neither is it uncommon to take on the responsibility for the abuser, to become the parent, the adult or the liable person in the situation.

The effects are not unique to this type of abuse, then, yet may have an added dimension in terms of implications for further help and therapeutic relationships. This may be from two angles. First, in that the therapist is now in the position of the former abuser from the client's perspective, so that the difficulties with trust may be acutely exaggerated. Secondly, a therapist may find it more difficult either to believe the account, or to deal with their feelings about such a reported case. Both possibilities have implications which will be explored at the end of this chapter, and both may become demystified through gaining more knowledge.

It is worth noting that there is still little research available which is based on the experience of the client, in the sense that they are the interviewees, the contributors to the debate, rather than the subject of clinical assessment. One of my objectives was to try to give a voice to clients who felt that they had been exploited, and, in looking at how they experienced the effects, to try to gain further insights. In looking at how they experienced these effects then, I will make some categorisations for the sake of ordering which I believe makes learning more effective. At the same time, I am cautious about making too finite a syndrome, particularly as some feelings and connections made may be elusive or hard to make tangible. The following findings then are presented very much in this spirit, of representing likely possibilities rather than definite conclusions.

Identified effects on clients

It seems that sexual exploitation within therapy is a process within which various boundaries are crossed. We need, then, to note the effects of this process and of the therapist's interventions *even before* the client has conceptualised them as exploitative, in order to understand the intricacies of the sense of exploitation. This may help alert both practitioners and clients to potential danger signs, and enhance our understanding of the strength of feelings involved.

Feeling special

One of the immediate effects of overtly friendly or flirtatious behaviour is that the client may develop a sense of feeling unique and somehow special to the therapist. The belief is that 'he or she only says this kind of thing to me, therefore I mean something to them'.

> By this time I was beginning to feel these feelings, which I now know as transference . . . wanting to be with him, falling in love with him if you like, but I didn't know it as that. What happened was when he used to come and get me from the waiting room I used to feel very special . . . and I used to walk past all the people in the waiting room, I remember feeling the feeling that it was *me* that was walking with him, he wasn't going with anybody else, it was *me*. And then when I would go in the room with him and he would say sometimes how beautiful I looked or how nice I looked, that made me feel ten feet tall and I thought oh gosh, this is lovely, I love this feeling and to get all the attention and all this, but again all this [transference] I knew later, I was completely ignorant at the time.

> And I mean he made it very obvious that he found me very attractive, and he would quite often make comments about that, and I just remember how I fed off these . . . well it's innocuous in a way but he shouldn't have said that.

Such feelings may of course be intensified by the feeling of illicitness that goes with them. Many participants reported knowing that the interactions which they found so appealing were somehow wrong as well. This sort of secrecy contributed to the feeling of uniqueness.

Any interaction which seems as if it singles out people in some way must be clearly motivated, as must the passing of a compliment. Even to say how good somebody looks may provoke issues of 'pleasing the therapist', whether or not there is anything sexual within it. Again, it would be difficult to make a prohibition of any 'humanness' within the therapeutic relationship, but it is my feeling that a great deal of caution needs to be exercised.

So, compliments and manner may have great impact on the client. Overt commentary will inevitably deepen the perceived degree of intimacy in the situation. The therapist is letting the client know that he or she has had some impact on the client, that is specific and unique to that particular client. If the compliments are ingenuine, then the therapist is being incongruent. In either case, I would suggest that a lack of respect is evidenced.

The effect of such interventions is a false sense of 'specialness' – not false in the sense of imagined, but false in the sense that the therapist is not in a position to offer such intimacy. The possibility is, then, that the client will begin to see the therapy as assuming facets which it really cannot live up to.

Dependency

Dependency is strongly tied in with feelings of love, and is another of those effects which needs to be seen as part of the exploitative process. Any dependency necessary involves a sense of disempowerment for the client, and this has to be extremely carefully worked with. To encourage or foster such feelings is not conducive to the client's needs, and can increase the sense of vulnerability which the client will already be feeling:

> I went through a stage of wanting him to leave his wife, I went through a stage where I was getting very dependent on X and he was always very loving and gentle to me.

There is a wide range of theoretical perspectives to the place of dependency within therapy, indeed as to whether it has a place at all. One end of the continuum is represented by the problem-solving model of counselling which emphasises the notion of empowerment and sees dependency as negative, whereas the other end of the spectrum is represented by some analytical therapy where it is seen as being an integral stage. Clearly in either case dependency is not something to be manufactured for the practitioner's own ends.

Trust

Every participant in my own research described a sense of betrayal of trust. This links strongly to the feelings of being special which have been identified.

One of the three male participants described a series of events which led him to question his own judgement and which he felt influenced his personal development. Having lived for many years in a culture where therapy is accepted as a norm, he had his first experience of it as a young teenager. This was in response to his difficulties following a bereavement and a near-death experience. Recollecting the period, he remembered that the therapist he saw was a family friend who subsequently tried to seduce his mother.

Later experiences threw up issues for him which he conceptualised as issues of transference. Having worked to his benefit with a Gestalt therapist for many years, he became aware of a deep feeling towards her:

> I was half idolising her, it was following a familiar pattern. But when I

raised this issue, it was like dropping a penny down into a bottomless well, you never hear a splash.

He persisted in his desire to work through this idolisation and felt that he received no response at all. The result of this was to contribute to a mistrust of his own feelings – 'what is going on, what is really going on here?' As he put it succinctly:

This kind of issue begins at a very subtle level, it's not just somebody full of lust.

He felt no violation of trust for this particular therapist, as he felt that there was no ulterior motive, it was more a question of her inability to confront transferential issues at all.

Subsequently, he worked with another female therapist with the expressed desire to work with the positive transference which he felt for her. She was his tutor at one point and he originally approached her for supervision, until they made a counselling contract. This is worth noting as boundaries were already blurred, and he acknowledged that he had perhaps chosen to work with someone who demonstrated this, this being an issue for him.

In expressing his difficulty with trusting her, he found the following response:

She said either you have to trust me or you don't. And I chose to trust her because I thought that what she had to offer was very great. . . . She repeated it many times . . . 'You have to trust me, you have to trust me'. And I felt that I was kind of mesmerised by her.

This participant had a very clear sense that he would not feel ready to end therapy until the issues of transference were worked out – 'I didn't want to be mothered any more, I needed to feel equal.' In practice, he found these issues to be ignored repeatedly. On terminating therapy, his therapist accepted gifts from him while refusing to work with the erotic feelings which he expressed towards her:

This was something I just wasn't prepared for, game playing in any sense.

In evaluating the experience, the notion of trust, of both self and others, was dominant. This participant was left with a degree of self-doubt, and a feeling of betrayal of trust:

I gave her my trust and she abused it . . . I was absolutely devastated by this.

In communication with this therapist some time afterward, he received acknowledgement that at least one aspect of her behaviour was 'inexcusable', thus helping him with part of the self-doubt.

These feelings were echoed again and again in the course of this research. It seems that there were two levels of what was happening in the process of abusive practice. Both may be connected to the trust invested in the therapist. The first aspect begins during the period in which the client is aware of something being ambiguous within the therapeutic relationship, and which generates confusion and self-doubt:

> I think it is terribly hard to put my finger on exactly what it was and so often it was . . . like . . . the wind in leaves, that kind of rustling that I could sort of hear or feel or pick up on and I couldn't exactly say what it was. I could never be sure whether it was me or him and because of the situation I was always much more inclined to think it was me, that it must be something wrong with me.

> The worst thing about all of that is that it made me unsure of my own feelings, it made me distrust my own feelings . . . until other people named it for me.

The second level of betrayal manifests in relation to others, where the consequence is impaired ability to trust anyone else, specifically authority or nurturing figures:

> It has had a lasting effect on me. . . . Can I ever trust a man? . . . I don't yet know the answers.

> I see it as an enormous violation of trust . . . I've now had female therapists for four and a half years, and I still don't trust them, I mean I don't trust. . . . I'm absolutely paranoid.

We can see that this goes wider than trusting specific role-figures into whole groups of people, for example men. This can have enormous consequences for an individual's personal life. Trust is the quality that enables us to have some sense of continuity with our lives, a sense of predictability. Not being able to predict another's actions leaves us feeling precarious in our own safety.

Guilt

Guilt may be seen as having two main edges. Many of the participants in my research felt guilty for a while, as if the exploitation was their fault. They experienced further guilt in talking through the experience with other people, as if they were betraying the therapist. This was sometimes felt if the client ended the relationship. Both senses had a paralysing effect and served to both further depression, and to enforce, or reinforce, poor or distorted self-concept:

> I was a bit like a rabbit in front of car headlights, sort of fixed and frozen

and a bit afraid. . . . I think a lot of it was quite self-punishing, but I think this is in line with the notion of people who feel bad about themselves and who do bad things to themselves, and if you have a history like mine it seems an awful lot of bad things have happened to me then I have kind of gone full circle. I think this was another one, I am terribly loath to say I played into it but I feel that in some way I must have done. . . . I don't think I was seductive.

I just went into a state of total shock again and self blame and it's my fault I am making men do this to me . . . what is it about me that makes men want to abuse me?.

I felt guilty that I was causing them problems and at the same time I felt they [the service] were mucking me about.

I am still struggling with the guilt at ending the sexual side of the relationship. At some level it feels like abandoning a needy, helpless child who doesn't understand and is totally bereft.

I thought I seduced X, I don't think he seduced me. I must say this, I felt I was the initiator . . . I just wanted to be provocative. I didn't know what I was doing really, it was a pattern for me.

One participant was a co-worker with her therapist, which made for great difficulties with boundaries. When conflict erupted within the organisation, she felt both trapped and guilty:

I would have to either betray myself and just agree with things that weren't true or if I challenged her, I felt so vulnerable . . . I was obsessed with her . . . I couldn't betray her.

Several people expressed feelings of how difficult it was to speak to me because of feeling that they were betraying their therapist. Feelings of disloyalty were declared, and some confusion. One woman felt guilty about her therapist's exposure when he was disciplined:

I felt like it was all my fault, which was really awful. I'd thought it was all my fault that he'd been found out, that he'd been through all this misery, but not how much it was his fault.

Feelings of guilt were often exacerbated by the secrecy surrounding the experience.

Anger

Anger seems to be one of the pivotal emotions in any loss experience, and this seems to be no exception. Many people experienced a deep sense of rage:

I think what I would really like to have done, I don't know, chucked a brick through his window, cut off his balls, I mean you know, real sort of

vicious . . . I don't know what to do with that, I had an easier time
forgiving the man who raped me . . . because he didn't set himself up as
any kind of therapist . . . I think this is a very lasting damage he caused
me.

This particular participant was in the process of deciding what, if
any, action she should take. I say that anger is the pivotal emotion
because it seems to me that it can be experienced in a highly
destructive sense, either in being turned inward, as in extreme
depression, guilt, etc., or in being displaced, that is, expressed
inappropriately. When this happens, it can be a very frightening
experience for all concerned.

The positive and appropriate expression of anger however can
have a liberating, empowering quality. Feeling angry at what has
happened reminds an exploited person that the responsibility is not
theirs, that they have a right to be angry *because* they have been
exploited.

Anger can go along with a sense of outrage at what other feelings
have been engendered by the exploitative behaviour:

I did get really angry, and I didn't want to see him for a while. . . . I just
felt dirty then because in a way what happened, I didn't realise this, it
had followed through what was gonna happen with my father . . . so then
I had a sudden thought . . . oh my God, you've been in a transference
over your father, I mean I thought they're separate people. I could tell
myself all this but I realised my God, that's awful, that's terrible, really
bad, so I was really fucked up by that and I believed I wanted sex with my
father, and I thought I didn't I didn't and I thought I did I did.

The anger at the therapist was closely tied in with a feeling of self-
disgust, partly through how this participant had made sense of the
situation through therapeutic discourse. This later proved to be
something of a turning point for her, but at the time led into much
confusion.

Frustration and helplessness

Many participants expressed a sense of frustration at not being able
to warn other people about their therapists. It is not uncommon to
experience a feeling of helplessness when the incident is difficult to
disclose anyway, and when making any public statement is open to
charges of libel.

I felt I had to tell or else I would be colluding in him abusing others, yet I
didn't feel able to.

I knew he would deny it all and that I would have to be able to prove it in
court.

Several participants expressed hope that through publicity, other people might be spared the pain that they had experienced.

Ambivalence

Several clients were left with very mixed feelings, both about the therapy they had received, and about the therapist under question. As I have noted previously, this is often the case in any exploitative relationship where there is an element of affection, or an investment of trust on the part of the exploited:

> The spiritual side was part of the relationship and I wanted to hang on to that. . . . One of the other things he did was introduce me to classical music, he would be very romantic, I was learning things from him and I thought that was all very well and good. . . . I feel he's my friend a caring friend. . . . I would still say he's one of my closest friends . . . it should never have happened.

Clearly such ambivalence must be respected and is perhaps a part of the re-integrative process. To dismiss an experience which someone has actively participated in, albeit from a position of vulnerability, can be invalidating.

One participant brought this out very strongly. In her situation, the offending therapist was reported by someone who found out, and the police became involved. This engendered some confusion and a great deal of ambivalence for her:

> I really wanted to tell them, but I didn't want to tell against him. . . . I suppose I just wanted to tell people that I was just really, totally upset, the fact that I couldn't see him anymore. But I wasn't going to be allowed to see him, because I wanted to say my view of things, that to me it had been beautiful.

At a later stage, this woman reconceptualised and no longer saw either the experience or the therapist as beautiful:

> After about four years, maybe, I went to see him . . . and I just thought wow, what the hell did I ever see in this guy. He gave me the creeps completely. It was really sad that it felt like that . . . he felt like a dirty old man to me.

It may be tempting to dismiss the former feelings in the light of the latter, but I am not sure this is correct. My preference is to recognise possible patterns without imposing a straightjacketed analysis. This participant captures that perspective when she says:

> It's taken me a long time to make any sense of it, because people who did know about it . . . used to make it out to be a really big scandal or be really horrified, and I couldn't relate to that . . . I wanted them to understand and they didn't. Many years later, looking back on it and

seeing it from a feminist perspective, I'm supposed to see it that I've been sexually abused and maybe that is the case but I can't put it into that mould either, because I always felt that I'd been very much part of it. I'd never been a kind of innocent victim.

This sort of ambivalence or uncertainty must be respected, while accepting that this itself may entail confusion and shifts in self-concept. Several participants felt that they were agents in the process and that this is not incompatible with seeing the therapists' behaviour as exploitative:

Obviously it was wrong for me, it wasn't what I needed . . . if I hadn't had that I wouldn't have had anything out of being in hospital . . . I wouldn't have had the chance to talk at all [but] if he could manage to give me time the way he did, he could have given me that time anyway, without the sexual stuff.

Poor or distorted self-concept

Feelings of worthlessness and low self-concept is one consequence of any exploitative experience. Feelings of humiliation and guilt provoke such experience. It may entail a specific distortion when clients come to see their sexual nature as dangerous. There seems to be a mix of guilt and anger internalised – 'this has happened to me, therefore I made it happen, therefore *there is something wrong with me*'. This may have particular potency for women within a whole patriarchal discourse where it may be suggested that women ask for abuse, through their behaviour, dress, etc.:[1]

So given my experience, what this behaviour of the psychologist has done is told me again that there is something wrong with me, that people want to hurt me.

This feeling of distortion, of being in the wrong, also relates specifically to the inability to trust one's own perceptions, as outlined above. An impaired ability to trust oneself may itself engender low self-esteem and confidence.

Isolation

Finally, it is worth noting that several participants felt very isolated by the experience and felt unable to tell anyone for a long time. Again, this links with my experience of working with other situational exploitation, where the factors outlined above make it very difficult for people to disclose what has happened, or what is happening:

I felt I couldn't tell anyone, that I was alone. I felt there was no one I could turn to.

I must stress the *terrific* sense of isolation of the whole thing. I had hardly any support and had made the promise of secrecy so that I wouldn't be thrown off my course.

These feelings were echoed within the process of research when participants felt relieved to be able to tell someone of the experience, or to hear of others' experiences through the networks now being set up. Even when recognised for what they are, the powerful feelings of oppression and shame can be paralysing and reinforce the sense of isolation. All the more reason to have the problem overtly recognised.

Specific and idiosyncratic consequences

Various specific behaviours and other consequences were attributed to the exploitative experience. We must retain some caution in making a direct link in the sense of blaming the experience for each ensuing action, in the same way that it is difficult to be categorical about any emotional cause and effect. On the other hand, exploitation must be seen as having a major impact on the victim's[2] life process and it must be recognised that it can have devastating effects, either of itself or as one in a long line of experiences.

The most marked types of behaviours related to the experience seem to be of a destructive nature, either towards others or self. One woman felt that anger she experienced towards a child was in fact displaced anger towards the exploitative therapist:

It's hard for me to say, but I mean I actually battered my baby and I really do think that this is part of the process.

This particular participant had experienced more than one abusive relationship and found it difficult to express anger. Her understanding of the exploitative practice took a number of years to develop. It is within this context that she sees herself as having felt a degree of anger which she did not understand and therefore did not know how to direct appropriately.

Some clients felt that the experience of exploitation reinforced a negative pattern of sexual behaviour. This seemed to refer specifically to the practice of entering into a sexual relationship in order to achieve some other end. However, the desired objective, for example, love or affection, was rarely achieved in this way.

I suppose what I wanted was for someone to pay attention, and to understand what was going on for me, give me encouragement, and make me feel good. And I think that's possible, to show an interest and that you really do care about them without having to be sexual. I think I carried on a pattern of thinking I could only get sex from people, I had a whole string of disastrous relationships with people before I met my husband. Yes it reinforced that, it didn't help, I had to work out for myself that I could get attention from people without being sexual . . . and not being able to value ordinary friendships.

This seemed to be particularly the case for women in the research who had entered therapy with this pattern in place, whether this was to do with previous abuse or not.

One participant was both client and trainee to the same man who made a physical assault on her within a therapy session. She agreed to keep the secret of the event under threat of losing her place on the course. When she eventually told what had happened, she was asked to leave the course, a decision which adversely affected her whole career.

Some participants experienced feeling suicidal and attributed this directly to the exploitation and the despair that went with it:

I remember screaming, literally, and I can't [usually] scream, the bastards, the bastards, why him too, remembering back . . . and then I had the weekend and was very distressed and suicidal feeling.

Two participants actually made suicide attempts following the exploitative therapy. This underlines the severity of effect when we realise and appreciate the context in which the client is operating, namely that often the therapist is not the first exploiter.

One participant was repeatedly exploited by her general practitioner who was offering her therapy and who repeatedly had sexual intercourse with her. The depression for which she was being treated deepened and she feels that this was instrumental in the ultimate consequence of her losing custody of her children. This participant also expressed suicidal feelings and a sense of deep helplessness.

Again, this is not an exhaustive list, more an illustration of the range of quite concrete effects attributed to a sense of post-traumatic stress.

Problems of subsequent therapy

For the client

The client is likely to enter subsequent therapy with many feelings which are left over from the experience. One difficulty may be with the ability to trust that they will be believed, understood and worked with in a constructive way. In other words, that they will be safe and validated. They may feel angry or resentful that they feel that they have to have therapy at all:

> Well I did have to go back and sort it out because I'd still got these bloody awful problems. He's complicated it now. I was a bit irritated, thinking Oh God why should this have happened. I told him straight-away, I said look, I've had a male therapist . . . and we ended up having an affair, I don't want it to happen again.

This particular client was able to be very assertive about her experience and her needs, and subsequently worked through the issues that she wanted to. Not all clients may have this insight and courage, however, and therapists must be alert to this possibility.

It is worth stating here that subsequent therapy is only one avenue for reparative work. One client draws attention to the inevitable power dynamic within therapy, and wonders:

> I'm not sure all therapy isn't some kind of abuse . . . now I'm doing co-counselling, I can see what's wrong with any kind of therapy . . . I understand about transference and dependency, it does make a person very vulnerable.

This particular participant is distinguishing between those psychoth-erapies with an ideological basis and a specific form of counselling. It is worth making the point, however, that therapy of any kind is not the answer for all people.

For the therapist

The subsequent therapist for an exploited client is in a highly sensitive and specialised role. The new therapist is in the shoes of the former exploiter, and will be expected to be ultra safe where the former was dangerous. He or she may be the subject of a great deal of hostility and must be able to handle this for what it is. Of course, the new therapist must be scrupulous about boundaries. Mistakes through insensitivity or incompetence will carry an extremely high cost in serving to revictimise the client.

It is likely that the client will be extremely suspicious, with reason, and thus the therapist will need to offer a genuine warmth and stability within which the client can develop trust at his or her own pace. It is possible that the therapist's interventions will be met with cynicism, disbelief or rejection – 'you're just saying that, why do you think that?' – and it is essential that the therapist is a clear communicator. Clarity of purpose is crucial.

In a way, this last seems obvious, and is a point that I have drawn attention to in Chapter 1. I would reiterate that no therapist has the right to inflict mystery or theoretical frameworks upon clients. It is the foundation of effective therapy that every intervention is purposeful and comprehensible to the client, and that every response from either side is checked out and clarified. This is so for all clients, and needs to be underlined in this situation in recognition of the extra dimension.

Subsequent therapists might find themselves in a situation where they have trouble believing the client. This might happen because of their own vulnerability leading to defensiveness, or a tendency to close ranks, consciously or otherwise, and feel protective towards fellow professionals. It might also occur if the account conflicts with their own model of therapy.

If this is the case and the issue cannot be resolved in supervision, then the therapist must refer elsewhere. This is obviously not ideal for the client, and can have serious effects. It draws attention to the importance of clear contracting at the outset, and continual, high quality supervision so that we as therapists know our limitations before accepting clients.

There might also be an attempt to want to use the therapist as an advocate, adviser, or judge. It is essential that any decision-making about whether to complain, or to confront the previous therapist, must be the client's own. Again, I would see this as consistent with any other therapy in the sense of being facilitative rather than directive, but it is worth being aware of the issue.

Clear boundaries entail having consistency of time and place and leaving no room for misunderstanding. The limitations of the relationship must be stipulated overtly. Clear boundaries must also be applied to the process of the session. Two people in my research were thrown, suspicious and distrustful when the therapist took phone calls during the session. This was seen as not only disrespectful, but might be construed as conspiratorial. Subsequent therapists must be aware of this.

Summary

The effects of sexually exploitative practice within the therapeutic relationship seem to follow a pattern not unlike that of other sexual exploitation. The findings of this research tie in with that of the American experience, namely, that it can result in feelings of guilt, sadness, anger, poor self-concept, and impaired ability to trust self or others. This in not an exhaustive list, rather a summary list appropriate for this context.

Behaviourally, these feelings may manifest in a variety of ways. Specifically, this seems to often entail destructive behaviour to self or others. We must also note that people may feel ambivalent about the whole experience and be sensitive to this. Should an exploited client choose to go for further therapy, he or she might find specific problems as might the therapist.

Notes

1 For more discussion of this, see such works as Vance and Snitow (1984).

2 I use the word victim for convenience in this context, in the knowledge that it carries negative connotations for many people. The intention is not to convey a sense of the individual as forever victim or helpless, but to indicate that in the particular situation they are victimised.

3

CLIENTS' ACCOUNTS

This chapter has one main aim and will be divided into two sections. Having looked in detail at some of the effects of abusive behaviour, the aim here is to try to outline with some coherency the *circumstances* in which clients felt abused – who they are, the reasons they went to therapy, what happened to them, how they felt about it and what they felt able to do. This is another format with which to angle the points made throughout the book, with the aim of validating the experiences and educating the practitioner.

The first section of the chapter will be subdivided into headings as described above, in order to group together the range of circumstances and experiences. This necessarily retains some fragmentation of stories and continues to protect anonymity. Hopefully, it demonstrates the range of behaviour and experiences which participants found exploitative.

The second section comprises summaries of one whole script where the participant (Jo) has felt happy to have this included in detail. Several participants offered this facility, and the responsibility for choosing one has been mine. Some of the material will necessarily duplicate occasional quotes already included in this work, but with the full context of the story rather than the headings I have chosen to focus on. In other words, this is another perspective to appeal to the reader, and in which to represent the stories – the wider the sincere audience, the better.

Participants

I asked very little information about the clients themselves, in terms of background, occupation, etc. One or two demographic observations may have relevance for further research in terms of who might have felt able to approach me.

All of the participants were white. As far as I know, only two were from a non-British cultural background. All respondents except for four were female. The method of my research is far too unstructured to allow for any conclusion or meaningful analysis of this information to be made. I include it really to add a little cautious speculation that perhaps as a white woman researcher I may influence who might respond. The subject area is so sensitive that I think any factors which might engender or discourage trust should at least be noted.

It is worth mentioning at this point that one woman who took part in the initial research later asked to withdraw. I have her permission to mention this as an example of how very difficult it is to share some of this material. She felt very strongly that the story was hers to tell and that there was a sense of loss which accompanied 'giving' it to me. There was also a feeling of wanting to have her account acknowledged without having to go through any professional channels. I can greatly appreciate this sense.

There were other people who made appointments to see me then did not turn up. One woman changed her mind four times because she felt so sensitive about 'betraying' her therapist, despite wanting to participate to argue for the retention of erotic touch as part of therapy. All of this may be useful to remember in designing further research or in any examination of the problem to hand – our information is necessarily limited.

My resources for conducting the research were, to understate the case, extremely limited. Nevertheless, I have managed to interview people in various parts of England and Scotland. It may sound obvious but perhaps needs stating that the problem under review is not confined to any one geographic area.

Reasons for entering therapy

The reasons for which people went into therapy were varied. Ascribing motives is one of those processes which changes over time. What we think to be an initial reason may with hindsight be reconceptualised as we develop new insight and receive more information. Participants' own words best capture the flavour of some of these understandings and perspectives:

> The thing that drove me to counselling was that I was having problems in my relationships with men, and this is what gets me quite angry really, I mean all he did was multiply my problems and he should have known better. . . . In retrospect I have realised that I'm a relationship addict . . . but I didn't know that at the time and what I went with was a problem with having had a long-term very difficult relationship . . . and with having an affair . . . and I hadn't got a child, I hadn't got what I wanted out of life and I seemed to be embroiled in all these difficult relationships, unfulfilling in many ways and very hooked into them as well. So that's what I went with. I explained all that in the first session.

I went for marriage guidance, my marriage was breaking up.

I discovered after I was untimely ejected from my parents' house in 1985 that in a period of about twelve months I had been sexually abused and I began to kind of suffer all the effects of that, the post-traumatic syndrome. . . . I had been told I was mad and mentally ill and disturbed and that had gone on from me being a very small child. . . . It wasn't till I gave birth to my first child . . . that it really hit me and I was in a dreadful state . . . exceedingly desperate, very very depressed . . . hurting myself quite badly, I had this baby I didn't know what to do with. . . . If I didn't find help I really was going to do something stupid . . . I would walk out and leave my family, or hurt myself very badly or hurt my child or hurt my partner because a lot of the time I was just out of control.

Very briefly, I had been abused as a child and then when I was 15, 16, I had an extremely abusive relationship with this bloke and I had had a breakdown and attempted suicide . . . then in 19XX this crisis I was in was reaching its peak [this participant was working in an agency which worked with abuse survivors] . . . and [the organiser] said that nobody should do counselling without having had counselling themselves . . . which was obviously very important for me because I knew that I had to look at my issues . . . I was thinking maybe I will just be able to offload a bit about the symptoms I was getting . . . this was like the biggest thing I had ever done in my life.

I think I'd had a lot of experience in my life of death, and near-death experiences, so a lot of anxieties and stress has been the result for me. I had a lot of hassles with my mother [*laughs*] and these are the main reasons you could say.

I felt at the time it was important to work with a man, I had been with a woman therapist some time before . . . but since one of the aspects of myself I wanted to explore was my relationship with and effect on men, I thought, perhaps mistakenly, even in principle and certainly in practice, that if I could establish a trusting relationship with one, safe man, I could explore a lot of incidents/behaviour in my life, including rape.

These give some indication of the range of reasons why people were seeking help and perhaps to help focus on what they might have expected from the therapeutic relationship. There is quite some variety, and differing degrees of desperation in these scenarios. It cannot be emphasised too strongly that people may come to therapy at a significant point in their lives, perhaps at a crossroads where empowerment to act is central, or perhaps at a point where they want to try to change patterns of behaviour. Often the client has had to summon up courage in order to make the first move. To be able to trust the helper is of paramount importance. Perhaps it is only through knowing the context and thus perhaps the degree of investment or the strength of expectations that we can appreciate how devastating it is to feel exploited in this situation.

Two points emerge here, one being to underline that it is perfectly reasonable for the client to expect safety, and it is always the responsibility of the therapist to ensure that this condition is not violated. Secondly, it is also important to be realistic about what therapies of different kinds can offer, to know the limitations and make these widely available to the public. Therapy is not a magical cure-all.

Expectations are, it seems, an important part of what we invest and what makes us feel let down. Some of the above excerpts have a certain air of desperation about them, or else represent entering therapy at a particular crisis point. Now this is the reality for many people. One of the points in this research which is of interest is the experience of the woman who participated to defend the potential for physical touch in therapy. She says the following about her own entry into therapy and about her apprehensions of the research:

> My reasons are . . . it's sort of knowing I needed therapy I suppose, and that took a long time to come to a decision about that, and on another level I was looking for a replacement for what I hadn't had in childhood.

Note that there is a leisurely feel about this and a fairly general issue for exploration – this particular woman was not in crisis at the point of entry. She goes on:

> It's the last part that interests me, how it [erotic contact] can be beneficial, and part of me doesn't want to deny that sexual abuse happens in therapy, although that's not part of my experience. But I was quite frightened by the clamour about it, afraid because if I hadn't had physical contact in my therapy from my therapist . . . I wouldn't be nearly as well or as far as I am now . . . I wanted to talk about some of the differences and why there's a difference.

It feels important to note this, and to look at what the differences are likely to be. It is perhaps significant that this was the only respondent still working with the therapist under question at the time of the interview with me. For her, the major condition that made erotic touch okay was that it was not made for the gratification of the therapist, and neither was it only erotic. This participant felt that:

> I'm using her sexually, she's not using me. There's been clear boundaries from her, even when there wasn't from me fantasy wise.

The touch was experienced as always negotiated, a means to an end rather than an end in itself, not for the gratification of the therapist, and in a context of clear boundaries. This seemed to make the difference for this client.

Another general observation is worth making here, again cautiously. Of the thirty-plus participants in this research who had been clients, about half reported previous sexual abuse. Some of them were aware of this at the time, whereas for others, memories or issues emerged either during the therapy in question or else afterwards, either in subsequent therapy or while trying to make sense of their experiences.

Now my sample is too small to claim any kind of representative status, but it does seem that at the very least we have evidenced a tremendous ignorance on the part of the therapists concerned. One school of thought goes so far as to suggest that clients should be routinely asked if they have been previously abused. This seems difficult to me for two reasons: first, that we start to follow one path in a rather directive fashion, and secondly, that simply to ask such a question may not have the desired effect – it can seem impertinent if not asked at the right time, and, more importantly, may not elicit an answer even if there is abuse. Clients may be unable to remember, or may feel too ashamed or guilty to be able to answer honestly. So there are drawbacks to this idea. Nevertheless, the spirit of the argument is perhaps useful, to be aware that any client, that is any person, may have been sexually abused in their past, and to be aware that they may carry a particular legacy from such an event or history.

What happened within the therapy

It is sometimes difficult to pinpoint the precise moment where clients felt that something inappropriate was happening. In terms of behaviours, a wide range is illustrated. They may be loosely classified as non-physical and physical. Some of course will entail the two.

First, the non-physical behaviours. One client with a history of sexual abuse was describing to her therapist some obscene phone calls which she had received. His response was to become hot and flustered and to comment that the man was obviously 'only having a wank, what's all the fuss about?' He then loosened his tie, removed his jacket and began to make phone calls within the session. This client felt that this response was disrespectful and emotionally abusive. She felt that this was particularly so when he knew so much about her own sexual history. Moreover, the flushing and discomfort that he manifested suggested to her that he was physically aroused, and she found this frightening.

Several participants described feeling attracted to their therapist, and in two instances where there was no physical contact it seemed that the refusal of the therapist to acknowledge or work with this constituted the feeling of exploitation:

I was having these feelings and I was feeling ashamed of them. [He cancelled an appointment at my home] and I now know it was because he knew that I was having these feelings for him and he couldn't trust me being here, or he couldn't trust himself being here with me at home, he couldn't cope with it. . . . I sent him this letter [and] he went completely mad, he was so angry with me, he said you have embarrassed me with the things you have written. . . . He said he ripped up the letter and he threw it in the bin. He said that's the best place for that. I have never felt so humiliated in all my life. He really made me feel like an idiot and he said that the letter showed him I was very dependent on him and that that was bad for therapy and that it couldn't go on.

A male participant had a similar experience with a female therapist. Despite his protestations of erotic and love feelings towards her, and his expressed desire to work with these therapeutically, this element of the relationship was ignored.

Other verbal interventions seemed to fall into the categories of explicit overtures or of expressions of admiration or flattery, sexual and non-sexual innuendo suggesting loose boundaries, sexualising material, and verbal assault:

And I mean he made it very obvious that he found me very attractive and he would quite often make comments about that and about what I wore.

Before we had finished the agreed period of counselling he said to me I don't know that we really need to do much more of this, I think it would be just as easy for you to take me out to lunch instead. So that planted something in my mind that there was this possibility of friendship outside of the counselling relationship.

He would erroneously misapply Freudian principles and say things like 'you want to make love to me, you want to give me babies', and was verbally sexualising what I presented, verbally pestering me.

He said 'I want to penetrate you and master you as one might a problem.'

Physical behaviours were many. They included clear physical assault, the eroticisation of touch when the client felt distressed, stroking the belly of a pregnant woman, kissing, sexual touch as a diagnostic tool, affairs which included many sexual behaviours:

He had just gone on and on about sex and he had touched me constantly and it got so that he was just touching me on my knee and then it got further and further up my leg and he started touching me on my shoulders and then further and further down until his hands were on my breasts and I had to take them off.

He grabbed my breasts and shook me for about thirty seconds.

During this session I became very upset and was weeping. He asked me to sit on the floor in front of him, my shoulders between his knees. His hands were on my neck, and then on my face which was wet with tears and as I tried to speak I could feel his hands were round my mouth, touching my lips, his fingers playing between my lips, in my mouth.

The circumstances of the particular assaults and abuses varied. One participant met her psychiatrist in hospital following a suicide attempt. She was at that time undergoing a course of electroconvulsive shock treatment. He suggested an affair to which she agreed and which was lengthy. Other affairs went on outside of the consulting room. One woman was assaulted in her own home when the therapist in question came to solicit her custom after she had made initial enquiries. In another instance, a general practitioner who was offering therapy went to a patient's home to have sex under the guise of a home visit.

We can see then that there are a wide range of behaviours which constitute exploitative practice. Some situations can be seen as inappropriate relationships, whereas others involve specific instances of abuse. It is much more than sheer sexual attraction between two parties in an inappropriate situation. The situations and acts vary in their degrees of subtlety or overtness, and it is noteworthy that the degree of perceived distress or damage to the client did not correlate to any sliding scale of verbal/physical behaviours. All had powerful and serious consequences.

How clients felt and what they felt able to do

The effects of exploitative behaviour have been documented in Chapter 2, and it is not my intention to duplicate this. It is worth reiterating some of the major points, however, to remind the reader of the impact of such behaviours. Key categories seem to be shock, disbelief, guilt, isolation, anger, responsibility for the therapist. As stated before, some clients experience ambivalent feelings in this situation. There seem to be two categories of response, immediate and long term.

Examples of immediate response include the following:

> For a few seconds I simply couldn't believe it. Then I went cold inside and the question formed in my head 'What the fuck is going on?'

> I just went into a state of total shock again and self-blame and it's my fault making men do this to me.

> I wanted him to do it and at the same time I felt very uneasy about it.

And examples of long-term response included:

> I felt so isolated. I was made to feel like [a] criminal. This is some years ago but I feel so furious about it I can't tell you.

> The long term effect is that I find it very difficult to trust men . . . I'm much more worried for my son than my daughter.

I'm still trying to work it out and make sense of it.

I felt depressed and suicidal.

How clients felt influenced, how they felt able to respond and therefore influenced what they felt able to do. As far as I know three participants made complaints without success. One is in the process of doing so. Many felt that the long-term consequences for them were serious, and felt very angry when talking about the experience. Some ascribed the cause of suicidal feelings or attempts to the process they had been subjected to, and one participant felt that it fuelled the depression which led to her children being taken away from her.

Many felt trapped in the web of secrecy and conflicting feelings which they were caught up in. The following long quotation, while not claiming to be representative, perhaps captures some of the emotions which several people felt. The specific situation here was a lengthy relationship which began in the therapeutic encounter and continued outside of it. The participant involved ended the relationship with much difficulty.

> I am still struggling with the guilt at ending the sexual side of the relationship. At some level or another it feels like abandoning a needy, helpless child who doesn't understand, and is totally bereft. I guess I am still not in touch with my anger, and not sure what to do with it in as much as I am. I am more aware of my (at times) overwhelming fear. I also recently talked with a friend with whom it transpired my therapist had a sexualised relationship as well. I can't tell you how liberating that was, hearing her describe all the feelings and conflicts I have had, including the guilt, protectiveness, and saying how persuasive she had experienced him as being. Although mostly I desperately wanted and needed the relationship, at the times I didn't want it, or didn't want to be sexual, I was totally unable to say no, or even get up and walk away. I felt paralysed. . . . To hear that my friend, with the same man, had done so helped me not to be too hard on myself. I have despised myself for letting him use me all those times.

Several people echoed the desire to talk to other people in a similar situation, or the relief of having done so. Some people who have had exploitative experiences, or who have a concern about the issue, have set up networks to support and help each other. The addresses of these networks are included in Chapter 8.

It is clear then that this issue is about serious misconduct on the part of therapists which has enormous impact and sometimes devastating consequences for the clients involved. Hopefully these accounts will help to alert practitioners and clients alike to the warning signs of exploitative practice. No client should have to go through such an experience in the name of therapy, *any* kind of therapy.

On that note, then, there follows the summary of one account of a woman who was exploited by her therapist. It is chosen from many as it exemplifies a lot of the complexities of such an experience. Being presented from beginning to end, its objective is to engender deeper understanding for all concerned. For reasons of anonymity, the name has been changed, as have one or two details which might lead to identification.

Jo's story

Jo began by telling me something about the therapist concerned. He was also deeply involved in an Eastern spiritual philosophy in which he was her teacher. Jo felt that this was important:

> I think that's another dimension to it, adds further screws to the screwing up process, you know, further turns of the screw because . . . you also have a relationship with your teacher and in a way you don't ask questions of it. You have to take what he says.

This particular counsellor had also been Jo's trainer as well as her spiritual teacher.

Jo felt that in this context students might have questioned some of the spiritual teachings but that they wouldn't question what he asked them to do:

> When spiritual development gets mixed up with sex some people had difficulties with that and there's a lot behind it that I don't know about, but it's another form of exploitative relationship that I feel quite angry about.

The therapist in question was not trained as a counsellor but in one of the other caring professions. He and his co-trainer had met at a counselling conference, and subsequently set up a business training counsellors:

> He had learned from her and then become a trainer in his own right, but he hasn't actually had any training except from his own sexual partner. . . . So he wasn't trained and hadn't had any therapy until recently. . . . So really he came in with nothing, with nothing to back him up really apart from his relationship with her and that he learned fast and is a smooth talker.

Jo did not know whether he received supervision or not, her impression was that he sometimes did from his partner:

> He isn't a bad counsellor at all. I think there are limitations because of what I call his sexual addiction, I mean that is what I am putting it down to, so he is limited there, and he is limited in that he doesn't believe in

transference and so he doesn't believe in his own responsibility for keeping anything that happens within the therapeutic relationship.

One of the frustrations which she felt was that this man was, at the time of interview, on a higher degree counselling course elsewhere in the country and that his examiners would pass him in ignorance of his particular problems.

Two things had led Jo to go for counselling with this particular therapist. One was that he followed the same spiritual philosophy, and the second was that the main problem which she wanted to resolve was to do with unsuccessful or unfulfilling relationships with men. He seemed as if he would be appropriate from both perspectives:

> I was either misunderstanding or there were inherent contradictions between [the spiritual philosophy] and the growth movement and I wanted to work that out, and I did work some of that out in the counselling and that was good. But the thing that drove me to counselling was that I was having problems in my relationships with men, and this is what gets me quite angry really, I mean all he did was multiply my problems and he should have known better. What I went with was a problem with having had a long-term very difficult relationship with one man that I was still in, and having an affair with a man who was married. He'd had a vasectomy and I wanted a child, I was about thirty-nine and I hadn't got a child, I hadn't got what I wanted out of life and I was embroiled in all these difficult relationships, inappropriate but I didn't feel that at the time. Difficult relationships, I wasn't getting what I wanted. Unfulfilling in many ways and very hooked into them. So that's what I went with. I explained all that in the first session and we started work. I had two blocks of counselling and in the first block he behaved impeccably.

As Jo said that, she expanded that he helped her a lot with issues around her father during a block of about twelve sessions. She remembered also that in the middle of that block he had said to her that she may as well take him for lunch as they did not need to do any more counselling, although they clearly had not fulfilled the contracted time and she felt there was more to do:

> I knew there was this possibility of a friendship outside of the counselling relationship, but I knew I had more to do and really that was inappropriate because I hadn't finished and it should be me who defines when I had finished and not him . . . so I ignored that remark . . . but I mean I did start to weigh up, well actually I weighed up the price and I thought it would be cheaper to go out to lunch than to have these sessions. Anyway, I finished the agreed period and I can't remember who invited who out for lunch, but we did go out for lunch maybe once a month and it was purely friendship which was great.

Jo became interested in the therapeutic effect of counselling and enrolled as a student on his course. She acknowledged how well she got on with the therapist, and went on to place him in a context where at his particular centre, both he and his co-director seemed to encourage relationships with clients and students. She felt that both were in some way dependent on these as she saw them as 'workaholics', so that there was some inevitability about the overlap into the social life.

Jo was subsequently involved in helping the therapist and his partner set up a venue for a residential course in psychodrama which she attended:

> So again you are friends as well and the client thing gets a bit lost by then, but then he approached me that summer in a very romantic setting, he sort of suddenly said to me 'oh I feel so much closer to you', and I said 'well I don't feel any closer to you . . . because I am trying to keep you at the distance I can handle you at basically', and he said 'well that's no excuse for not being close'. I said 'yes it is' and left. That was sort of quite straight that I didn't want to be any closer, but I was also admitting that I could only handle him at that distance so I gave a little bit away there because I was aware of an attraction, and was trying to learn to be more honest.

Jo subsequently went for more counselling around the theme of her relationships with men. One of the issues within this was the discovery that her lover had been sexually abusing his daughter which had been a great shock. The other was the tendency to be involved in unfulfilling relationships.

At some point during this second block of counselling an issue arose which Jo wanted to discuss, to do with relationships in the work setting which she had some strong feelings about. Rather than using counselling time for this, she invited her counsellor for dinner:

> I felt very angry, I felt it [his behaviour] was really irresponsible, so we talked about all that and then he just took hold of my hands and kissed me. . . . I feel embarrassed and a bit ashamed that I just caved in so completely and totally, I put up no resistance at all. . . . Then he took me round to his place and we didn't actually have intercourse as I couldn't really settle down to it. . . . So I had one night and during the course of that he told me that he had listened to a tape on visualisation and he said that in this tape you had to visualise what you really wanted out of life and he had visualised me in his bed, that was what he really wanted. . . . Looking back I would say that it was the attraction of him in the counsellor-role, the attraction of the power thing over quite a long time, that led me to give in so quickly.

Jo mentioned that she was struck and appalled by the difference between the non-directive style which he advocated and the very directive style of his sexual activities.

Following the sexual encounter, she cancelled the next counselling session and began a struggle with boundaries as she valued her friendship with him. She subsequently had a second sexual encounter at a residential weekend meeting for the spiritual philosophy. On this weekend she met another woman who was a student, ex-client and spiritual follower of the same man and who told Jo that she too was having a sexual relationship with him:

> So all the warning bells went, I thought hang on I can't actually believe what he is saying to me.

Jo later discovered that there were other involvements and that there were similarities in the pattern of seduction experienced by each woman. One of the women who later became openly involved with him subsequently became a co-tutor, 'so there are two tutors there openly demonstrating that it is okay to have a relationship with a client'.

Jo next went for therapy with a woman, and got in touch with the memory that she had been sexually abused as a child.

> So I have just been repeating the pattern and this was just one of the repeats and that's what screwed me up. I should have been able to see this by the time I had been having an affair with a man who I then found had abused his own daughter, you know, an experienced counsellor would have been on the ball. He didn't know about my own abuse, but I think it didn't come up because of the relationship we had. . . . So I feel angry that we couldn't work with my patterns within the counselling and that they had to be acted out, basically I acted out my patterns instead of keeping them within the boundaries of counselling. . . . Now two years later I am allowing my feelings to come out about it. . . . That's why it's disturbing me now really, it's because he repeated the pattern and I wanted help to come from telling someone. I feel betrayed and yet it has taken me a long time to get to the feeling of betrayal and even to talk to anybody to get help about it. And that's the other question, what do I actually do?

Jo had found it difficult to get to the point of talking about the events at all.

> I felt that I was betraying him, complaining about it all . . . it has taken me a long time to talk to somebody like you about it and I know that's the case with sexual relationships, you seem to be very loyal to him. I struggled for ages feeling I should talk to him about it but I am frightened, I am afraid that he might turn up at the house when I am on my own, I am afraid of actually facing him on my own.

Jo found it very helpful when she read about other people's similar experiences, and this affirmed her right to feel betrayed and her understanding that the boundaries should have been kept by him, that it was his responsibility to do so.

She was left feeling unsure how to take her own case further, and very concerned that he is practising as a counsellor and trainer with an unethical perspective. At the time, she considered making a complaint to a counselling organisation but found the telephone response unhelpful. She was told how to make a complaint and that it would have to be in writing, but at that point had felt she really needed discussion first. There was also a difficulty in that he did not, at that time, belong to a particular professional body.

When she first spoke to me, Jo felt frustrated that she seemed to have no avenue for confronting the therapist involved. Subsequently however she managed to confront him face to face. A year on since the initial interview for this book, Jo has decided to make an official complaint as she heard that he had applied to a counselling body for accreditation for his course and his training centre. She is supported in this by another woman who feels similarly abused, and finds that in making the complaint she has had also to name those who were collusive in the whole event. This perhaps highlights how there are often more people involved (or seen to be involved) in exploitative practice than the named exploiter.

Comments

While not claiming that there is any such thing as a typical pattern of exploitation, these accounts illustrate vividly some of the major themes which seem to be repeated. They show how therapists who abuse often blur boundaries in other ways and abdicate responsibility for the sexual boundary. Often there is a lengthy interactive process which operates, and subsequently it can be seen that power issues, and the magnetism of power, play a central part. Exploited clients are left feeling angry and betrayed, and feel helpless as to what to do. They also show great strength in the courage which they exhibit in trying to deal with the issues concerned. Professional bodies are seen to be only minimally helpful at present. It is my hope that the accounts will help to change that situation.

4

THE THERAPISTS

> This woman I took to be very lonely, I got the impression she'd been alone for a very long time.

No therapists participated formally in this research from the point of view of feeling that they had transgressed the boundaries and exploited clients, although I have had discussions with many practitioners about the blurring of boundaries. The work then is heavily dependent on the client's perceptions and interpretations. This does not devalue it in any way, and there is a certain welcome irony in the situation in terms of depending on the clients' view for our material. Nevertheless, this gap reminds us that there is more work to be done in this area.

Clients' observations are augmented by my own theoretical perceptions, and by research which has been conducted in the United States. Much of this work attempts to make a profile of the offending therapist and of the most common scenarios. In making my own perceptions, and in keeping with the spirit of this work, I will try to relate individual aberration to a wider context within which we can work.

In interviewing participants, I asked whether the therapist was privately or publicly employed and financed, what school of therapy he or she belonged to, and if the client knew whether the therapist was supervised. I was given much more information than this, however, as a part of the clients' trying to make sense of the experience and of the ambivalent feelings which they frequently had.

The American profile

Research in the United States has been used to offer a profile of the offending therapist as likely to be male, to have undergone personal therapy, and to be accredited by a professional body (Gartrell et al., 1986; Herman et al., 1987). Bouhoutsos (1985) found that 90 per cent reported feeling lonely, vulnerable and needy at the time of the malpractice. She also reported that once having had sexual relations with a client, 75–80 per cent are likely to repeat this behaviour.

There are many exceptions to the male–female dyad within the research. Sonne et al. (1985) found that three respondents in a women's therapy group had been sexually involved with female therapists. Gartrell et al. (1986) found that two male offenders had themselves been involved with their own male therapists. Masters and Johnson (1970) reported female therapist–male client, and male therapist–male client combinations. Coleman and Schaefer (1986) found 10 per cent of a sample of 350 clients reported sexual relations between female counsellor and male client, while Bouhoutsos (1985) reported more male client with male therapist dyads than female–female.

Gartrell et al. (1986) also reported that therapists who had sexual relations with their clients were most likely to 'treat' previously involved clients. This may suggest a referral network between sympathetic therapists, or a greater sensitivity on the part of the offending therapist which may encourage disclosure by the client. It is also possible that therapists offend after finding out that the client has been involved with the former therapist, a pattern recognised as not uncommon to victims of abuse – the confessor becomes the next offender. As one of the participants in my research suggested, 'I thought Oh God, he's joined the queue of abusers.'

It is a common finding that therapists who have sexual relations with clients will rationalise their behaviour (Marmor, 1972). Defenses take the form of denial, claiming that the client has consented to the contact, seeing the behaviour as therapeutic, justifying the contact on the grounds that it takes place outside the therapeutic hour or after termination of the therapy, claiming that the relationship is a love relationship, or pleading a loss of control or unguarded impulse (see Hays, 1980; Gartrell et al., 1986; Pope, 1986). These rationalisations are remarkably similar to the techniques of neutralisation observed by Martin (1984) in his study of major hospital inquiries into violence towards inmates.

These are the major findings of the American research with respect to offending therapists. There are also recommendations of how to deal with them or to help them. The profiling outlined above supports the view that the offending therapist is seen as impaired or distressed (Pope: 1987). This leads to assertions that further research into the psychodynamics of the offender would be useful as (he) is seen as dysfunctional (Gartrell et al., 1986; Pope and Bouhoutsos, 1986). Note how we are immediately within the language and discourse of therapy in how the problem is couched.

Bouhoutsos (1985), however, admits that we do not know

whether either psychotherapy or supervision for the offending therapist prevents recidivism, although these are the usual conditions for reinstatement by licensing boards in the States.

Treatment, training and education are the favoured avenues for eradication of exploitation and rehabilitation for the offender. Some concern is expressed over treatment as a way of escaping censure and ensuring protection and immunity (Davidson, 1977; Karasu, 1980). In terms of training, it is widely suggested that therapists' sexual attraction to clients be a subject for training programmes, that therapists keep up with literature, have better supervision, and that therapists become educated about the harmful effects of sexual intimacy within psychotherapy (Gartrell et al., 1986; Pope, 1986; Derosis et al., 1987).

Bouhoutsos notes the 'extensive sexual involvements between faculty and students in mental health training institutions' (1985: 181). Pope (1987) advocates a generally wider acceptance of sexual feelings in the self, to be worked with as a potential resource in therapy, and presumably this is to be so at all levels of therapy and training.

Pope and Bouhoutsos (1986: Ch. 12) offer a comprehensive checklist for both therapists and clients, to be used in order to prevent sexual intimacy between them and to prescribe the undesirability of such behaviour. They also offer a list of likely scenarios in which the therapist will offend. These are:

- Role-trading, where the needs of therapist become paramount.
- Sex therapy, where this is fraudulent.
- As if . . ., where the therapist sees transference as personal.
- Svengali, where the therapist creates dependency.
- Drugs, used as part of the seduction.
- Rape, where physical threats or force are used.
- True love, where the clinical nature of the relationship is ignored.
- It just got out of hand, where the therapist cannot deal with the emerging emotional closeness.
- Time out, where the therapist discounts the clinical relationship outside of the office.
- Hold me, where the therapist exploits the client's need for non-erotic physical contact.

Two perspectives are offered in analysis of therapists who abuse. Therapists are seen as distressed, as needing therapy (for example offending male therapists need to work on the relationships with their mothers), or as power hungry. The research quoted above lends support to the aberrational individual point of view – therapists will only offend if they are in some way dysfunctional. When they do offend, it is by concrete nameable actions for which they will need help.

Where researchers locate the practice in a wider social context, it is within the patriarchal discourse and seen as an expression of sexism, 'the tip of a sexist iceberg' (Karasu, 1980: 1510). Phyllis Chesler, one of the earliest writers on the subject, draws attention to the predominance of male therapists and 'the resultant tendency in psychotherapy to replicate within the dyadic relationship in the "one down" position in which women are typically placed' (1971: 363). Chesler suggests that this replication functions similarly to marriage, as a vehicle for 'personal "salvation" through the presence of an understanding and benevolent (male) authority'. In this analysis, help comes through being '(expertly) dominated' (ibid.: 373).

This is a radical analysis and offers no explanation of the alternative dyad abuse. On the other hand, it is useful in helping us see exploitation as occurring within a social context, and not in a vacuum, also in seeing it as a continuum concept rather than sudden or separate acts. Some research suggests that male colleagues protect known offenders either by silence or by treatment, and by not challenging 'facile notions' (Davidson, 1977: 48).

Such notions may incorporate the concept of a double standard of mental health existent for men and for women. This is best illustrated by the classic study by Broverman et al. which found that 'Clinicians are significantly less likely to attribute traits which characterise healthy adults to a woman than they are likely to attribute these traits to a healthy man' (1970: 5). They speculate that such practice arises from an 'adjustment' model of mental health, so that the mentally healthy woman is one who is adjusted to her environment even where it might entail behaving in a way which is considered less socially desirable than for a 'healthy mature adult' (ibid.: 6).

Chesler, in pursuing the theme, questions whether women can ever really benefit from therapy with a man, asking: 'How free from the dictates of a sexist society can a female as a patient be with a male therapist?' (1971: 385). This reminds us of value systems operating within the mental health profession which must be addressed, and sexism must be one of these factors. My own perspective is that it can be fruitful for women and men to work together, while sharing absolutely the belief that sexist practice not only exists but can be detrimental in the long term.

However, I would reiterate that male-exploiter–female-exploited is not the only dyad where we find exploitation, and there is as yet little attempt at explanation for this in a wider context. It is also worth remembering that Broverman et al.'s findings applied to female clinicians as well as to males. I found no consideration of class or race as potential variables within exploitative relationships, presumably because the focus has been on the sexual, so that gender becomes the obvious consideration. As within sexual abuse generally, however, the radical feminist perspective has limitations as well as the insights which it offers.

Finally, and following on the above, the American research has looked at aspects of collusion and of reporting. The documented attitudes of practitioners towards sexual contact between therapists and clients is educational, and a major area for consideration. Extensive research by Herman et al. with psychiatrists suggests that the 'majority of psychiatrists have knowledge of such cases but do not intervene' (1987: 164), despite the finding that 98 per cent of them believe sexual contact to be inappropriate during or concurrently with therapy, and that 97.4 per cent believe it to be always harmful.

Their complementary study, however, found that only 8 per cent of psychiatrists who had clients who reported sexual contact with a previous therapist then reported it, and only 6 per cent of those who knew abusers reported them (Gartrell et al., 1986: 60). Over half of the respondents thought that reporting should be made mandatory. One possible explanation for the discrepancies may be that mandatory reporting diminishes the sense of dilemma and responsibility that accompanies decision-making – to believe that we have no choice may be a relief.

Holroyd and Brodsky's study (1977) found that 70 per cent of male and 88 per cent of female therapists thought that erotic contact would never be beneficial to the client. Kardener et al.'s study (1973) had found that 20 per cent of psychiatrists held the view that erotic behaviour may be beneficial. Clearly, beliefs as to the desirability of the behaviour is a key issue here, and it would seem that these findings indicate differences of opinion depending on gender and school of therapy.

Holroyd and Bouhoutsos' study investigated the possibility of bias in the reporting of sexual behaviour by professionals:

> The most significant result of this study is that psychologists who reported that patients were 'unharmed' admitted approximately three times the prevalence of sexual intimacy with their patients as did psychologists in the population at large. This is despite the fact that within the larger sample, the prevalence of therapists who had experi-

enced sexual intimacies was the same as found in earlier surveys. (1985: 707)

This would suggest that the incidence may be underreported. It is arguable however that the incidence generally may be overreported depending on the motivation to respond.

The issue of reporting becomes complicated. Two sides of the argument seem to predominate – one is that knowledge of what is perceived to be an abuse of the therapeutic relationship should always be reported to the professional body concerned, with or without the agreement of the client if he or she is the source of the information (Morrow, 1987: 12). The other is that confidentiality is sacrosanct and must be the essence of the decision-making process (Shapiro, 1987: 11–12). Often the conflict may be between the rights of individuals and the greater good of the many. Disclosure of abuse without consent may be experienced as another betrayal of trust.

However this may be, what is suggested from the data so far available is that a large percentage of the professions involved in therapy are cognizant of the practice of sexual contact in therapy, are likely to know at least some individuals involved, think it to be ethically untenable and harmful to clients, yet do nothing to intervene or to challenge the practice. This is despite findings that although 'offenders' mostly thought that patients felt predominantly positive about the sexual contact, 87 per cent of therapists treating previous therapists' 'victims' saw the effects as *always* harmful (Gartrell et al., 1986: 1129). This suggests the possibility of a large network of peripheral people involved in the process of this 'deviant practice'.[1]

Therapists – my own research

As I have already stated, when I have discussed this with fellow professionals, the reaction has been quite muddled – yes they knew about it in the United States, but surely not here (just as someone in Sussex once said to me that they knew child abuse happened in the north, but surely not here!). On reflection, however, several did know someone who 'it' had happened to. It is fair to say also that some practitioners are only too aware of the problem and concerned to change it.

Various practitioners talked to me about their own dilemmas, of feeling sexually attracted to a client, or of being unsure, when they liked a client, whether it was ethical and desirable to have *any* kind of ex-therapeutic relationship. One practitioner talked to me about his having had a sexual relationship with an ex-student which at some point had had a counselling dimension. My information then depends largely on clients' perspectives or on informal discussion with practitioners. So how do we see the errant practitioner in Britain, then, and what are the attitudes towards them and to sexual contact in therapy?

The therapists in my research spanned a large variety of therapeutic schools and philosophy. I asked all participants if they knew what kind of therapy was practised, and what they knew about the training and supervision that went with this. Responses varied from having a very clear idea of the therapy concerned to not really knowing what they did, just knowing the professional role.

> He was a social worker, he wasn't trained in counselling and he set up business with his partner . . . and she was trained. . . . Really he has learned from her and then become a trainer in his own right, but he hasn't actually had training from anybody other than his sexual partner . . . they were person-centred. . . . He had very informal supervision with her . . . he is now doing an MA in counselling.

> She was a marriage guidance counsellor . . . and certainly I knew at least three marriage guidance counsellors who were having affairs with their clients.

The span of disciplines represented included a general practitioner, marriage guidance counsellor, Community Psychiatric Nurses, Jungian therapists, psychoanalysts, psychosynthesis, Gestalt, bioenergetics, 'touch therapy', person-centred counsellors, re-evaluation counsellor, and 'counsellors' – 'he seemed to be eclectic'. Four were female and the rest were male. There were two complaints about one of the female therapists. There was also the female therapist whose client participated to argue the value of the erotic within the therapeutic relationship.

Clients made their own assessments of the therapists and their motivations. It is perhaps enough to illustrate the client's overview of those concerned.

> He isn't a bad counsellor at all. I think there are limitations because of what I call his sexual addiction.

> She really was the anima figure which I had spent my life looking for . . . she was a very charismatic lady, strikingly attractive, and she had a kind of warm vitality which I think I now recognise as some kind of persona. . . . I suppose as I got to know her better I came to see that actually she was extremely vulnerable, and terribly frightened.

This last participant saw the therapist as both incredibly powerful and tremendously vulnerable. She had recently lost her husband, and this client wondered whether he was seen as some sort of replacement.

It was not uncommon for clients to perceive areas of loneliness or need within the therapists' lives. This ability to understand, to somehow see the inadequacies without judgement, is again reminiscent of the legacy of those who are exploited in other situations. This perception was often fed by the therapists sharing what *was* going on in their lives through inappropriate self-disclosure.

> I told him that night that I was very attracted to him, and then he said that he'd had an affair before, and he'd just come out of this affair, and he said 'I've got a lot of problems with my wife'.

> He was always very easily led, I would say, I didn't have to say or do very much. He was very needy, very needy, which doesn't sound like what you're talking about really.

One of the difficulties for some participants was in seeing the therapist as the abuser. The above quote illustrates this, and again I would take note of the difficulties of terms and labels. Just as all participants did not want to label their experience as abuse, so they did not want to label the therapist. Again I would refer to some of the myths that sexual abuse is a specific act carried out by an aberrational person. The terms abuse and exploitation are being used to elicit meanings and to develop insight. The exploiter is the ordinary person, perhaps a kind and caring person in some ways, and it is this which needs to be taken on.

There are also instances of therapists who are discovered to make a practice of exploiting their clients. This seemed to be seen in three possible ways: as yet further manifestation of the vulnerabilities or needs of the counsellor; or as opportunism and deliberate, repeated abuse; or as poor practice on the part of the practitioner. In the first two conceptualisations, it was sometimes identified as occurring in the context of other blurred or transgressed boundaries.

For example, three participants referred to the therapists in question as being some sort of cult figure, or relationship junkie. This referred to situations where the therapist seemed to make their whole social life from those who had been clients or students, a social life wherein they had a higher status:

> I didn't want to live in this little claustrophobic world which was dominated by one individual, like a little religion or something.

> It is person-centred counselling, they encourage friendship because they are massive relationship addicts, they are workaholics as well. So they don't have appropriate relationships outside of their work so they are dependent emotionally on the students and clients for relationships really . . . they haven't got a social life outside, and that's one of the problems, they are not clear themselves on the boundaries at all.

In this second instance, one of the therapists in question was known to have had sexual relationships with several clients, and subsequently cohabited with one.

Where the therapist was seen to be operating poor practice, the understanding seemed to be that they were operating as therapists who did not really have adequate training or support:

> He had had no training, and received no real supervision. He was the Community Psychiatric Nurse then, and I didn't know what kind of therapy this was, I didn't even know he was a CPN, he called himself a therapist. I don't know what kind of therapy he was doing, he never told me, I know now that it was psychotherapy, which he had not trained to do.

In these instances, it seemed that the therapists in question did not know how to handle either the material under review, or the relationship which developed between them and their clients.

Where the therapist was seen to be opportunistic, it seemed that they had become known for having several inappropriate relationships or for behaving inappropriately as trainers with some regularity. One of the therapists involved was, ironically, a trainer whose one-off workshop I had attended myself. This was at a conference of trainers and I was 'tipped off' that he was a 'touch dodgy'. This meant that he was known for inappropriate sexual touching under the guise of therapy.

Opportunism was not exclusively related to (known) repeating offenders. One participant recalls:

> I saw X for a chat – he mentioned the common male difficulty of having 'affairs', and being afraid of the wife finding out.

At later dates, she remembers him telling her that there were plenty of other patients who he could have sex with if he wanted, and that:

> sex was like a Chinese takeaway – you feel hungry, you eat, and then you feel hungry again.

As far as she knows, she was the only client to be sexually involved at this time.

As yet, we seem to have few ideas on suggested remedies for therapists who overstep the boundaries and exploit clients. Several people commented that the therapists had not yet had their own therapy, or that they were 'unworked out'. This is not a point that I picked up during interviews, so it is my own inference that there is perhaps a belief or suggestion that therapy for the therapist would help. This certainly echoes the American perspective offered above.

Training and supervision are also referred to by clients as being lacking in the therapist. Again, this suggests that they would be believed to make a difference. This may reflect the bias of my interviews in the sense that I asked whether therapists involved were having supervision. The response seems to be that there was a real mix – some 'don't knows', some who were and some who were not.

In the United States, there is a clear commitment to the *rehabilitation* of offending therapists. The favoured method is to appoint two mentors with clearly differentiated tasks (Pope, 1989). One is to act as psychotherapist to the therapist, the second to help the therapist to develop professionally in order to minimise further risk.

As far as I know, there is no forum in Britain for therapists to be rehabilitated, should that be thought to be desirable. One participant in my research had been approached in her role as counsellor by a therapist who disclosed repeated instances of exploitative behaviour. At that time she felt very isolated in this knowledge and ignorant of what might be available. I wonder whether or not this is a common experience.

At present there is no central register for therapists in Britain so that it is difficult for them to be struck off, should that be appropriate. The United Standing Conference for Psychotherapy is, I understand, pushing for legislation so that action can be taken against those who do exploit. The British Association for Counselling is also looking at the possibilities of a registration system.

In terms of a wider viewpoint, discussion and experience seems to indicate that many practitioners know of other practitioners who transgress boundaries and exploit clients. For most, there is a real dilemma about what to do about it. Many people expressed discomfort with the idea of doing nothing, as if they were colluding with the behaviour under question. Others did not know what to do if the client involved did not want to make any complaint.

It seems to me, and this is subjective yet informed speculation, that there is a mixed view among British practitioners. There is, to begin with, some ignorance of the problem under review. Secondly, there sometimes operates a disbelief that the problem exists, or that it could be of any significant size.

Thirdly, there are practitioners who know that the problem is there but are unsure whether or how to act. Many believe that sex with clients or students is damaging. Some believe that where adults are involved, there must be scope for sexual relationships and that it is not damaging. Some simply see it as nothing to do with them, a kind of distancing technique. Many would differentiate between a blatant sexual assault (for example a physical grab) and a sexual relationship. This reflects a particular conception of what constitutes sexual exploitation or abuse.

There is, then, some confusion and at least some collusion operating within the British therapy networks. This perspective is echoed by user groups, often much more forcibly than this. It seems to me that it would be useful to conduct a methodical research enterprise to glean more information on this front in order to establish a more accurate perspective.[2]

Conclusions

My own perception on the therapists, at a second-hand level, fits none of the stereotypes commonly offered in terms of abuse. It seems unlikely that they are made up of evil opportunists, setting out to lure and abuse clients. It seems equally unhelpful to see them as people who will abuse only at certain low points when actually they are in need of therapy – for example, if their marriage is breaking up. It seems narrow to adopt a pathological view which takes no account of the ethos of therapy or of the political climate of its practice and context. In other words, at least some of the behaviour under review reflects sexist, heterosexist and exploitative attitudes which are common to the society in which therapy is practised, and to the professions involved.

My perceptions are rather more complicated. At one end of the scale, I would accept some deliberated opportunism, here as in any walk of life. I would also accept some level of distressed practitioners. I would also see an element of poor practice by people who are really not skilled or experienced enough to be doing the job. However, in the majority of instances, it seems more helpful to conceptualise this in terms of blurred boundaries. This seemed the case in many of the respondents' stories. Since sexuality is a powerful aspect of our condition, then it is likely that some boundary transgressions will be of a sexual nature.

This makes for an understanding where at least some of the exploitation that occurs is situational. In other words, the person is taking advantage of, or actively seeking out, a forum where various conditions make for potential exploitation. The types of individuals who abuse this potential will vary widely, and many may exploit in this situation and not others. Again, more research is needed to clarify the picture.

Notes

1   See Lee (1969) which illustrates that in deviant practice there are many hidden participants involved. In this case the process was securing an abortion, but the point made may be transferred.

2   As far as I understand, there is currently only one completed piece of research at present in Britain. In a survey of 300 clinical psychologists, it was found that 4 per cent admitted to sexual intimacy with current or former clients, 22 per cent had treated clients who reported sexual intimacy with previous therapists, and 40 per cent knew of offending therapists through sources other than clients (Garrett, 1992). Further details are yet unavailable as this work is at present unpublished. Clearly such research in Britain is currently in its infancy.

5

SEXUALITY – AN ELUSIVE TRILOGY

> I found him attractive and we got on very well and we laughed
> a lot together, but what I was aware of all the time in the
> sessions was I had always kept him at a distance, I mean I
> wouldn't have too much eye contact with him or you know, all
> the things that would develop into a sexual thing I made sure
> didn't happen.

As stated at the beginning of this book, central to its theme is an
understanding of what is meant by sex and sexuality. I have
contended already that proscriptions to sexual relationships within
ethical codes are limited by their inability to clarify what is sexual.
Thus it is difficult to specify the ban in terms of attitude or
behaviour.

The client quoted above draws our attention to the ambiguity of
'all the things that would develop into a sexual thing'. The tendency
in all the major works on this subject is to limit the term to a
physical, largely coital, relationship between therapist and client.[1]
This has been echoed by the reaction of other professionals to
whom I have spoken. This understanding is challenged, however,
by some of the people involved in this research, a challenge which
needs to be addressed by the professions involved.

One of the major consequences of having a limited understanding
is that clients in the exploitative relationship often doubt whether
their experience is valid. Several participants asked me for reassur-
ance that the experiences did indeed constitute an abuse or an
exploitative relationship if there was no overt sexual assault involving genitals, or if they felt they had colluded in some way.

Rather than try to fit those experiences into a pre-existing
paradigm or definition, I would like to use them to enhance our
learning and understanding as to what might constitute, or be
experienced as, sexual. In other words, I would like to discover
rather than ascribe definitions.

To provide some framework, then, I would like to look at four
facets of sexuality under separate headings. First, the social construction of sexuality; secondly, the personal construction of sexuality; thirdly, some psychological theories of sexuality which may
inform the therapist; and finally, my own paradigm of sexuality

which will suggest some of the features of sexual exploitation. The aim will be to clarify our understanding of how we conceive of sexual boundaries being crossed, and what behaviours we see as contributing to this conceptualisation. This may help with both preventive practice and reparation.

Sexuality as a social construct

> Nothing is sexual but naming it makes it so. (Plummer, 1975 in Weeks, 1986: 25)

Sex and sexuality have been much discussed within sociological, historical and feminist literature over the last twenty years or so, and it would be useful to tap this discussion to enhance our understanding. It seems that we might benefit from a multidisciplinary perspective. Perhaps the first place to start is with clarification of the terms.

The term *sex* is frequently used as if it suggests a shared understanding, as for example in the much used expression 'safe sex'. It is worth noting however that this word is both historically and culturally specific. It had been traditionally used to denote the physiological characteristics of the person – what sex you are, male or female. At various points in history, we can find evidence of sex being used specifically and absolutely to mean women, as a sort of derivitave of 'the fair sex' (Heath, 1982: 8–9). It is currently seen as being different from gender, which is seen as denoting behavioural patterning and attitude.

The change in meaning to incorporate sexual *practice* has really developed over this century. According to Heath (1982), expressions such as 'sex life' and 'sex appeal' emerge in popular parlance around the 1920s. This starts to develop the concept of sex as being rather more than physiological, but assuming certain life styles with all the values and attitudes that this entails. One's sex life will be denoted by what type of sex we have, how often and with whom. Sex then becomes a commodity, something we can like or dislike, choose or not, and something we can 'have'.

The notion of sex in this sense gains official recognition in the 1975 version of the *Oxford English Dictionary* (*OED*), primarily to denote coitus, its use meant as 'pertaining to sexual instincts, desires or their manifestations'. This suggests an essentialist view of sexuality, that is to say, one which focuses on drives and instincts and which forms the basis of the dominant Western view. This seems to revolve around certain conditions and expectations, namely, that heterosexual coitus with orgasm is 'full sex', and that anything else is foreplay, substitution or perversion.

We can see straightaway how this usage feeds into the blur around what makes an experience sexual. As stated above, one of the common understandings of sexual exploitation is that it means having sex in the terms outlined above, namely, heterosexual coitus. Another is that it should at least involve primary or secondary sexual characteristics.

However, it is clear from the experience of participants and from our wider knowledge of sexual exploitation that 'the sexual' denotes much more than this. There is in fact a value system operating around the concept which has nothing to do with physiological urges, needs or experiences. Indeed, such definitions operate more as a constraint than as an enabling conception, and can give rise to misunderstanding.

In the study of sexual abuse, it seems relevant to ask the question what is sexual about it? For most participants, it would seem that sexual exploitation incorporates the idea of a motivating factor being sexual stimulation or gratification for the perpetrator, not the victim. The victim may or may not be sexually aroused by the activity. This seems to be a reasonable working concept.

Further, although the experience may or may not be sexual for the victim, it may become sexualised through its symbolism, or through its consequences. So that in the case of penetrative rape, for example, the symbolism may be to do with the perpetrator claiming some aspect of the victim's sexuality which he or she may then internalise to produce, for example, a fear of being able to feel sexy or sexual in public places.

We can see how this essentialist and physiological notion of sex delimits and debars in non-exploitative situations. For example, for those without fully functioning sexual organs, in the physiological sense, can we assume that there will be no sexual interest of any kind, and possibly stimulation and gratification? Another example is the experience of male orgasm. Several men I know are able to experience an orgasm without ejaculation, and ejaculation without orgasm. Both may be seen as sexual in one sense or another, and this is perhaps the point. There is more than one understanding of what makes something sexual, of sex.

It seems pertinent, then, to widen our terms and to see the sexual as that which involves not only sex but *sexuality*, a wider and less definitive concept. In exploring this term in workshops, we come up with a myriad of attitudes, experiences, behaviours, self-images, societal images and expectations which may come under the heading of sexuality. In one sense, it serves to denote certain attributes of our being, yet in another, it seems a nonsense term in the sense that it is *inseparable* from our very being. One participant in the research, upon discovering that her therapist showed a sexual interest, felt 'wonderful, marvellous', and this is a feeling that many of us will have had.

I would suggest, then, that the term and concept of sexuality is itself a construct, that is to say that on a cultural and individual level, our view of and experience of sexuality is set within a total context of how we see the world and ourselves in relation to the world.

It is this which is culturally specific. Sexuality in the sense of the human experience of the sexual has been everpresent throughout history. The emergence of the *term* sexuality in the Western world however is recent. It first appears in the *OED* in 1800, to denote not only sexual behaviours, but such concepts as sexual feelings and sexual powers. It is a term of conception and of systemisation of a whole range of experience and attitude, an attempt to represent the sexual.

As Heath points out the difficulty is in using the word *sexuality* with all its assumptions in that second sense without making claims that we are talking about the first sense, that is, all human sexuality (1982: 11).

For example, take the case of how Western society sees children's sexual development. Crudely speaking, we know that it is common for toddlers to play with their genitals. They may encounter a variety of reactions, ranging through prohibition, laughter, encouragement or non-interference. The reaction may be gender specific, for example many adults seem to find little boys playing with their penises, more funny than threatening, while the reaction may be vice versa for girls.

At any rate, children quickly learn what is acceptable to the adults around them, and this will shape their behaviour and experience. They will in the natural course of events want to know where they come from, and again will encounter a range of reactions. At some point they may receive sex education, wherein the dominant ideology will be expounded. A certain age is designated as where it will be reasonable for them to have sexual relations with another, again the age will depend on the sexual preference expressed. The media by now will have had some impact as to what sexual fantasies should be, how they should dress to be sexy, etc. The list could go on.

The point is that when we say that sexuality is a construct, what we mean is that we can look at it as being formed through a series of representations – words, images, myths, medical discourse, etc. We attempt to order what we see as the sexual, and in the ordering we feed into a process where the ordering influences the criteria for being sexual.[2] In other words, we are told *how to be* sexual, with all the norms that this involves.

This is a relativistic position, and the danger within it is that it then becomes impossible to include or exclude any behaviour from the category sexual. In practical terms it then becomes desirable to recognise and acknowledge that we do inhabit a specific culture, and that it is therefore encumbent upon practitioners to adhere to certain norms of behaviour, to recognise that a kiss, any touch which includes the primary or secondary sexual characteristics, any touch that is motivated by a subjective feeling of desire or urge to sexual gratification, or any intervention that is thus interpreted by the client as sexual, are out of bounds.

The whole sexuality debate is a huge area and it is not relevant to take it too much further here. There are two major points which have specific relevance however. One is the *mode* in which sexuality has been constructed in Western society, and the second is the *means* which have fed into the construction. In simple terms, we can say that the mode has been as a problematic, and that the means of the construction are largely psychological.

Sexuality and psychology

In a way, this work is self-referential to the idea of sexuality as a problematic. Both my perspective and the participants' experiences bear testimony to it. So what does this really mean, and how has this come to be? Crudely speaking, it means that sexuality has become an accepted concept which needs to be worked at, worked out and explored. The means of doing this are more or less loosely tied up with therapeutic perspectives, and there is contention that sexuality is, at least to some degree, a mental process or attribute.

Michel Foucault (1985) is a major source of documentation as to *how* psychological practice has been instrumental in problematising sexuality. He argues against the commonly held repressive hypothesis, namely, that matters of sex had been repressed from the seventeenth century onwards. In this analysis, Victorian society is seen as representing the pinnacle of repressive practice and prudishness. Foucault turns this argument on its head.

On the contrary, he states, during the three centuries under question, we saw a veritable explosion of concerns and debate about sexuality, and related it, significantly for counselling, to the confessional. There was pressure, arising with the Church and culminating within psychoanalysis, to disclose and share all our innermost thoughts, particularly about sexuality. Indeed, he contends that this is where the conceptualisation and naming of the term sexuality originates.

Now, Foucault's challenge to the history of sexuality is to suggest that rather than moving from liberation to repression, the discourse of sexuality moved from repression to permissiveness. The means by which it did this was, during the eighteenth century, medicinal discourse, and, by the nineteenth century, through the discourse of psychiatry:

> What is peculiar to modern societies, in fact, is not that they consigned sex to a shadow existence, but that they dedicated themselves to speaking of it ad infinitum, while exploiting it as *the* secret. (emphasis in original) (Foucault, 1981: 35)

Medicine, psychiatry, pedagogy, are, for Foucault, mechanisms of power, and it is in relation to power that he conceptualises sexuality – sexuality is the site of a set of relations, either with oneself to the world, or oneself to another or to others. This is crucially different from the essentialist viewpoint described above. In other words, sexuality is another forum for the acting out of relationships.

Within this context, early specific usage of the term sexuality originates in medical discourse. Stephen Heath (1982: 1) names James Matthews Duncan as one of the earliest posers of the problem. In a set of lectures on the diseases of women, Duncan apparently stated : 'In removing the ovaries, you do not necessarily destroy sexuality in a woman'. At this time there appeared no clear concept of what this might represent. It might have referred to sexual feeling, attractiveness, fulfilment – it simply is not clear.

It is in this climate then that Freud was able to publish *Three Essays on the Theory of Sexuality* in 1905. Here we have the overt beginnings of a construction. Sexuality was conceptualised within the matrix of normality and abnormality. Sexuality was a problem to be solved.

Psychological theories have, then, dominated attempts to explain and understand sexuality throughout the last century. Freud epitomised the idea of a normal sexuality based on instincts and drives. His thinking, albeit frequently vulgarised, had an enormous impact on twentieth-century thought. Heterosexual intercourse became the pinnacle of sexual development and experience, all other sexual forms became symptoms of arrested development. The possibilities of incest were denied, the preference of homosexuality was perverted, and this of course had enormous consequences.[3]

Various theories have followed Freud. Wilhelm Reich, who stated that 'sexuality became aware of itself in the person of Sigmund Freud' (in Heath, 1982: 51) focused his life's work on the importance of the orgasm as the ultimate releasing life experience. In a way, he can be seen in context to the sexologists who followed, sexology being seen as a new discipline especially for the study of sexual attitude and behaviour. The work of Kinsey (1948; 1953) did much to add to the developing fascination with what is normal sexual behaviour, as did the work of Masters and Johnson (1970). Currently, Shere Hite (1977) must be seen as having a major impact on our understanding of what women and men want and how they get it. Classics such as Alex Comfort's *Joy of Sex* (1974) and *More Joy of Sex* (1977) (recently revised, presumably to add new angles) now grace the shelves of mainstream booksellers.

During this process, various forms of behaviour have gone in and out of fashion. Homosexuality in Britain was illegal until 1967. The right-wing backlash of the 1980s has seen various moves afoot to control the civil rights of homosexuals. Masturbation has gone through a change of status in the psychological literature. Seen as a perversion for many years, some psychologists now see a failure to masturbate on the part of adolescent males as a sign of maladjustment.

Psychological theories of sexuality took on a new twist mid-century, in suggesting that there were now therapeutic techniques which could be diagnostic as well as reparative. One participant experienced this approach at its crudest:

> He was putting his hand on my thigh . . . and I went like this [*closes thighs*] and I was getting very distressed about that. . . . And then he said 'Well, that's obvious you were sexually abused as a child' . . . and I thought about that, I don't know whether I was or not, but I think so.

This participant only returned for one more session after this incident and remarked:

> I felt he was so limited then in his diagnosis, it was a very very sexual situation always. I know this is only hearsay, but a friend of mine who went for individual therapy with him for two or three years said that he used to say to her 'You can't get away from the fact that I'm a man, you know, I've got a penis in here', and I think that's what was coming across from him all the time.

This type of therapy is clearly an abuse of the theories available, but we must also see that theories of sexuality, sexology and sex therapy even in their most ethical form impose notions of normality and deviance. What I am suggesting, then, is not only that sexuality is a comparatively new concept, but psychology and therapy are the major instruments for its construction and maintenance.

Thus we will find a different understanding of what constitutes the sexual in different societies, at different periods. In the practice of therapy, it is perhaps as well to distance ourselves at times from a narrow perspective.

This area is worthy of much greater debate, and the interested reader may refer to some of the texts referred to in this chapter. The point here is that there are no clear boundaries to sexuality or to what makes something sexual in terms of behaviour – it is mode and context which are the salient features. Within any therapeutic situation, then, both therapist and client will have their own understandings which are culture bound. The therapist will also be influenced by any theoretical knowledge they may have, as will the client. Both will also bring to bear their personal construction of the world and their values within it.

Personal construct of the world

There are two main elements to how we personally construct the world, which are relevant to how we conceive of our sexuality. One is to focus on how we interact with the world around us, another is how we construct our own value systems within that.

It seems that everyone has a need to make some sense of the world around us, and an interactionist perspective on this is one wherein life is seen as:

> chiefly a vast interpretative process in which people, singly and collectively, guide themselves by defining the objects, events and situations which they encounter. (Blumer in Plummer, 1975: 5)

Thus we give each other labels, we construct an understanding of people's roles, we have predetermined expectations of situations, based on interpretation of our previous experiences and information gleaned.

Roles are particularly salient to this work, in that role-inappropriate behaviour is only possible if we have a concept of role-appropriateness. The interactionist perspective acknowledges that people construct 'images' of how they expect themselves and others to act in given positions, an activity referred to as role-making and role-taking. Thus in a therapeutic situation, the client has expectations pertaining to the role, regardless of the person occupying it. This is demonstrated in the following comment from one client: 'I thought a therapist would be safe like a priest.'

A client entering a therapeutic relationship, then, may not only have expectations of what sexual dynamics might or might not go on, but will also have a concept of his or her own sexuality which is grounded in interactions to date with the outside world. Thus if told that he or she looks attractive, for example, the client may interpret this as sexual or not dependent on previous experiences. One theme that recurred was the notion of seductiveness, and the feeling in some clients that they had been seductive; conversely, several of the women in research were *told* that they were seductive.

> And then I got into this where he kept saying, 'd'you know, sometimes the way you look, it's quite seductive. You may not be aware of it, but that may be one of the problems, you're transmitting a message.' And I sort of knew what he meant, but I was muddled up.

Whether or not an individual believed this or accepted it would be directly related to previous experience and how it had affected self-concept. Where clients felt that this was in fact an insight which they wanted to work with, it was all the more reason for the therapist keeping very clear boundaries:

> It was what I wanted – I wanted him to touch me. And here I was acting out again and it was *so* important that he didn't respond.

> And perhaps I did give a message, typical things that people who have been assaulted think, it must have been something I was doing, and there are things like I need to be held, . . . I need to be touched, and sex is the only way I can get comfort . . . and I really opened up, talked about my sexuality.

This acted as an enabler for this particular participant, and later fuelled her anger at the subsequent exploitation she received from the therapist.

In looking at how we construe the world around us, it may also be useful to note the relevance of personal construct theory. This psychological theory formulated by George Kelly (Bannister and Fransella, 1986) has various philosophical underpinnings. The major postulate is that people have a wide variety and range of ways available to them to make sense of the world. He suggests that:

> all our present perceptions are open to question and reconsideration and . . . that even the most obvious occurrences of everyday life might appear utterly transformed if we were inventive enough to construe them differently. (in Bannister and Fransella, 1986: 5)

Two points are worth drawing attention to here which may go in line with the two major aspects of the theory. One is that the ability to construe means that we can constantly re-evaluate experiences by adopting another perspective, dependent on how we construct them in the light of new experiences, and in the light of new understandings which entail changing value systems.

For example, in this study the process of re-evaluation was common to many participants:

> I didn't feel he'd abused me at first . . . And then it suddenly hit me [as this client developed insights into previous abuse] this should never have happened, and it also hit me that while I was right in it [having just been abused] and really looking for closeness and comfort, and knowing that he *knew* that the only way he could get close was through sex, I actually felt really angry then. . . . And although I was seductive, he should have had the control.

The second major point in Kelly's philosophical theory is a recognition that values exist and are created in a social context. In terms of what is sexual, for example, our understanding of this will be highly influenced by the messages around us. At some point, this may be in conflict with our own experiences. Fransella and Dalton (1990) comment that many women's groups, for example, focus precisely on the concept of (re)construing, as women might have been encouraged to construe themselves as women in a man's world. The process of reconstruing may be freeing and enabling from some of the constraints that this imposes – for example, 'nice girls don't have sex', 'attractive women wear make up', 'women don't drive buses', etc.

More specifically, I would suggest that it is this social context which limits and constrains our understanding of what is sexual, with the result that confusion may arise between constructs and experience. For example, popular imagery emphasises the primary sexual characteristics as sexy; sex, as mentioned above, will commonly refer to heterosexual coitus. However, we may experience a look, a comment, a touch on the shoulder as an eroticised experience, but it may be difficult to say what was sexual about it in the popular and rather narrow terms which we are used to.

So for example in this study, many people found it difficult to put their finger on the first inkling that something was experienced as sexual:

> It was like grasping at straws in the wind. This seemed to begin at a very subtle level.

They also had some trouble fitting their own experience into common definition.

> I don't know whether you'd call this sexual abuse, he never actually had sex with me.

This may be different from your other participants, we didn't actually have sex in the consulting room.

Moreover, for the same reasons, it might have been difficult to conceptualise something as exploitative *at the time*, as the experience would be construed differently in the light of its consequences.

Previous experience will also have affected how participants construed events. For people who have been previously sexually abused, there is a whole range of confusions and ambivalences which might affect personal construction. One not uncommon consequence of sexual abuse is the tendency to confuse or conflate sexual attraction with love or affection – sex becomes a means of obtaining both:

It was a pattern I'd fallen into, using sex to get love and to boost my self-esteem.

I think this is the sense in which several participants construed the sexual side of things, either in interpreting the sexual as loving, or as using sex as a means of obtaining affection:

I was so needy . . . I was just starting to see how it was maladaptive behaviour and how it was *stopping* me from getting close to people . . . I needed to make people come back, it was like getting my mother back, my father, being loved.

Sex can also be used as a means of acquiring power or status where self-esteem is low:

I was being sexual with men in order to have a sense of control or power, and the thing is I never had any feelings for myself, I did it for them, almost like I had to be the active partner and they were the passive partner.

It is precisely at this stage that an opportunity arises for the therapist to help the client break old patterns. As stated above, this is where the boundaries need to be held extremely firmly.

Interpreting the sexual as affection is one mode of behaviour which leads to confusion and vulnerability. Another is the inability to say no. There may be internal or external pressure on a client to please the therapist. Subsequently, it may be that the therapist is construed as good, therefore it is the client who is, at the polar opposite, bad, or at the least, responsible.

There is a sort of continuum which operates here in terms of complaisance which connects to both the personal and the social construction of sexuality, and it is in this area that perhaps many therapists need much more education. In working with women over the issue of sexuality, for example, it has been my experience that wanting to 'please men', is a major message for some heterosexual women, and many will have had a sexual encounter when they have not actually wanted one. One woman said:

> For me there was always this tremendous desire to please him, so I would never ever like to confront him about anything that I felt was not right.

No doubt there are specific pressures on men to use sexual activity too, and the intention is not to seek victims–oppressors, but to aid understanding.

It must also be remembered in working with abused people that the urge to please at one's own expense applies to more than the sexual. Loss of trust in one's own perception, and loss of a boundaried ego identity both have a part to play in reducing the ability to be assertive.

We can see how personal construction is relevant here, both in terms of the self and in the sense of how the therapist is construed. On a scale of 'right'–'wrong', for example, the client may well see the therapist as always right. Authority and expertise is not only claimed but also ascribed by the client.

From the therapist's perspective, personal construction and value systems also operate. They too have former experiences and perceptions which bring to bear on how they make sense of a situation, what potential options operate and which decisions to make. As mental health work and therapy is heavily informed by psychological theory, this introduces another influence on the therapists' construction of sexuality, both in how they might see their own and the client's, namely psychological theories of sexuality.

So the individuals concerned will be operating a complex set of ideas, feelings and thoughts around the area, some of which are congruent with each other, some of which are not. How the therapist uses their power, how able the client is to be empowered will be the ultimate influences on whether or not the therapist exploits. The idea of congruence or incongruence seems to me to be helpful to an understanding of the more grey areas of exploitation, where intentionality and reception might blur, or where impact is different for each party concerned.

A tripartite construct of sexuality

It may help to see sexuality as a construct of a tripartite nature. As far as we can concretely conceptualise, I suggest that the main components comprising sexuality are that it is to do with a physiological urge and response system, that it is an aspect of self which is stimulated by a set of techniques, and that it has a spiritual side, not in the sense of Godly, rather in the sense of transcendence.

To exemplify, let us look at the act of coitus as a focus for analysis. This is not to conflate sexuality as a behaviour, rather to use such behaviour as one means of expressing our sexuality. Neither is it to see coitus as an ultimate expression as is so often claimed in Western society. It is rather that using such a focus enables us to tease out the three components more fully.

The physiological cycle is clearly demonstrated in coitus, through the patterns of arousal, stimulation and climax, whether or not all take place and whether or not in that order. The set of techniques is present in behaviours which provoke such a physiological pattern. This might involve a specific touch, the use of sexual material, a look, or any combination of a number of stimuli. The spiritual union, I would suggest, is symbolised by such notions as giving and receiving of pleasure, trust, a sense of own and other's worth, etc.; by the experience of penetration, being inside someone, containing someone, the invitation to enter; by the notion of possessing and being possessed; and by the sensation of the urge to devour or to be devoured.

This last aspect is perhaps near to Fromm's theory of erotic love as a transcendence of the self (ego). Fromm (1974) sees the psychological function of such a love as to break down the ego self and transcend it to form a greater union. He sees erotic love as seeking fusion, overcoming separateness. In the moment of that fusion, there may be a loss of self-consciousness which feels like a losing of self. This idea is reflected in language, such as wanting to be inside each other, making each other 'melt'.

To extrapolate from the focus of coitus as an activity, we see that such components are present in much expression of sexuality. Its symbolism remains in the kiss, in the interchange of fingers, orifices, tongues, etc. In sexual activity between two or more people, it would seem that one or other or all of the three elements are present in the shared expression of sexuality. One or more elements may be dominant at any one time, and this may or may not be in sync with the partner(s).

This seems particularly important in conceptualising sexual exploitation – the same activity may tap into different parts of different people's sexuality. A physiological urge in one partner, demonstrated technically, may be experienced or interpreted as spiritual by another. Some women describe the experience of not being physiologically stimulated or sated by their partners, but feeling that they want to share sexual expression as a means of expressing love. Some of the quotes by participants above demonstrate a similar process, in this case using sex (physical) as a means of obtaining comfort or affection (spiritual gratification). What makes an experience seem sexually exploitative is often described not only as physically violating, but also as spiritually so. Such a feeling seems to relate to concepts of trust and self-worth.

If sexuality comprises the three elements suggested, then it may be accepted that there may be a mismatch between the people involved. The variable that will then determine whether or not a sexual experience is exploitative is that of power. Where there is power imbalance, then the most powerful person(s) in the relationship may use a range of techniques from force to subtle coercion to obtain their own gratification. It is power differentials which make a sexual dyad inappropriate.

What seemed to happen for the participants in the research was that they felt exploited when their identified need which was of a mental nature – for example, developing greater insights, wanting to change patterns of behaviour – was responded to in such a way that some aspect of their sexuality was offended or exploited. In the case of non-verbal behaviours, it would seem that either the therapist experienced or appeared to demonstrate a physiological response to a sharing of material, or that they failed to recognise the degree of the spiritual element of sexuality aroused in their client. In the case of physical abuse, there seemed to be two main areas of mismatch. Either the client was overtly physically assaulted, or else a spiritual need was temporarily gratified by a physical and physiological response. All of these behaviours are exploitative because of the power differential.

With this in mind, then, it would be useful to give some examples of what participants in this study experienced as sexual. In terms of behaviours, there was a whole range: kissing, hugging, verbal interactions, denial of sexual elements present, physical demeanour, fellatio, sexual intercourse, bodily touching, body grabbing, inappropriate dress. They rarely occurred in a vacuum, and more often in a context which either made them, for the client, sexual, or which led for reinterpretation of previous interventions as sexual. All involved a blurring of boundaries.

Where there was an instance of erotic contact which felt non-abusive, it was the boundaries which made the difference as far as the client was concerned. She felt strongly that any physical contact was initiated at her request and fulfilled *her* needs and not those of the therapist. It was talked through and understood as a means to an end and not used as an end in itself:

I'm using her sexually, she's not using me. . . . There's been clear boundaries and limitations from her, even when there's not from me fantasy wise.

For this participant, the intimate physical contact which she craved, which included stroking and close holding, was an opportunity to experience the closeness she felt she might have liked from a mother. She felt that her control of the process enabled an equalising of power so that the physiological, technical and spiritual sides of her sexuality were stimulated and merged together.

Conclusions

To summarise, then, I am arguing that there is no such thing as one sexuality or a finite concept of what constitutes sex. It is too simplistic and misleading to confine the terms to denote the physiological or the essentialist view of sex. Our understanding of what our sexuality is will differ from culture to culture, and from person to person, dependent on their experience of the world. This makes for problems with making specific bans within the therapeutic relationship.

On the other hand, it must also be recognised that we operate within a specific Western culture, so that it would be reasonable and ethically desirable to concede to the norms of this culture. It might then be reasonably expected that any behaviours which involve either primary or secondary sexual characteristics will be seen as sexual. Any behaviour within a therapeutic relationship which is motivated by the sexual urge or for the sexual gratification of the therapist will also be seen as sexual. Any behaviour which stimulates the client into sexual response on any level may be seen as sexual. This makes it possible to preclude firmly such behaviour as kissing, touching of breasts, nipples, thighs, bottoms and genitals. It also makes it possible to alert therapists to the fact that *any* behaviour which makes them feel physiologically aroused is dangerous, and to alert the client to the same point. To have no recognition of such prohibitions allows a relativistic position to obscure the possibility of firm guidelines.

It seems that some behaviours of a sexual nature will be initially tolerated and even enjoyed by the client. This seems to work where the client is seeking a particular fulfilment which he or she conceptualises as sexual in some way. Later reinterpretation may add a different complexion to events where the client feels that a mental or spiritual need has not been met, but has rather been exploited for the physical or mental gratification of the therapist. This is possible precisely because sexuality is a complex construct and may acquire different boundaries for people at different times.

Notes

1   See for example Rutter (1990). Rutter's analysis is set within a Jungian framework, and within a patriarchal framework – in other words, it is about men abusing women.

2   See the last chapter of Heath (1982), or Weeks (1986), or Foucault's *History of Sexuality* (1981) for more discussion of this area.

3   See for example Szasz's (1971) exposition of the scapegoating of homosexuality. Masson (1984) provides some analysis of Freud's inability to deal with the realities of sexual abuse.

6
POWER

He enjoyed the power in the relationship.

Several participants in this research talked in different ways about the power in the therapeutic relationship. It is this which leads to the experience being framed as exploitative. The concept of trust is central here – trust may be abused when one party is in a position of more power than the other. Equally, exploitation may occur when the sexual needs of both parties are different but the power of the therapist enables his or her needs or desires to dominate those of the client.

The concept of power is rarely defined. Like sexuality, it often implies that there is a shared understanding yet it entails a range of assumptions and theoretical underpinnings which may differ from person to person. It is useful to tease out some of the conceptualisations and to make a little more explicit what I understand by the term power. Like sexuality, the chances are that this will mean accepting the complexities rather than having a clean understanding.

It seems that there are three main areas to be looked at here – one is in creating a working understanding of what we mean by power, the term. The second is to look at power in relation to therapy, in both its theory and its practice. The third is to put these together in an effort to understand these dynamics and therefore to be able to work with them in a constructive rather than an exploitative fashion.

Power – a working conceptualisation

The concept of power has long fascinated the socially inquisitive, and is the subject of many a lengthy tome. For the purposes of this work, it will be sufficient to draw out some summary points.

It is common for both professionals and lay people to talk about sexual abuse as an abuse of power rather than of sexuality, and 'power over' is a term often used in the exploration of exploitative practice. Peter Rutter, for example, who has researched exploitative practice between professionals and clients in the United States, contends that:

> highly eroticized entanglements can occur, behind closed doors, in any relationship in which a woman entrusts important aspects of her physical, spiritual, psychological, or material welfare to a man who has power over her. (Rutter, 1990: 1)

This overview does not quite capture the fullness of some of the findings of my research, in as much as some of the more direct and clumsy exploitative practices had no erotic content for the recipient. It also states the whole problem as one of heterosexual male exploitation, which hinges on a patriarchal model of power. While this has its uses, it seems to me to offer too narrow and static an analysis.

To explore this, the notion of 'power over' needs, I think, to be slightly challenged and drawn out. I have no doubt that there are situations where one party (single/multiple) is in a more powerful position than another. Several variables will influence any one situation, and gender may be one of these. Nevertheless, what strikes me is an old insight that one of the central facets of power is that it is not only exercised but ascribed. One participant in my research, for example, stated that:

> Fear is there quite a lot, I am not quite sure what I was afraid of, but of the power I gave him, I'm not very sure about all of that. But I think I did give him power. I think I probably felt, quite wrongly, that if I wanted to work through the things . . then I had to trust him, and I had this erroneous notion that I had to allow him power in order to do that.

This allowing or ascription of power may be for all sorts of reasons, but as a general point it leads to the realisation that power is not an 'it' that you either have or you do not have, power has a dynamic aspect that is pertinent to the *situation*. So, for example, a person may leave the family, where as senior adult and money-maker he or she exercises considerable power, and enter the doctor's surgery feeling powerless – powerless over his or her own body and powerless in the sense of how to handle it. The doctor is ascribed power because of his or her (perceived) expertise.

This example introduces some of the major aspects so far documented in the conceptualisation of power. One of the classic works on power is Weber's *Economy and Society*, which highlights this key point that power is a dynamic. Weber offers two definitions of power – he uses it to mean both:

the possibility of imposing one's own will upon the behaviour of other persons. (Weber, 1968b, Vol. 2: 942)

and

the probability that one actor within a social relationship will be in a position to carry out his own will despite resistance. (Weber, 1968a, Vol. 1: 53)

There are subtle and significant differences between the two. The first alludes to a possibility of direct imposition *upon* another person, whereas the other is allowing an individual to act as they like despite the behaviour of others, and despite resistance. The first is about influence, whereas the other incorporates force necessary to counter resistance. This introduces the dynamic force as power is not only about imposition, but about resistance. We may impose our own will upon someone else and we may resist both the will and the resistance of others – in other words, power gives us the choice of whether or not to comply with others, as well as the possibility of making them complaisant with us. Disempowerment suggests an inability to resist.

Moreover, power does not have to be seen as an imposition, it can be seen as an energy force, as a potent-ial. How and in what circumstances we exercise our own potential or potency will vary with time and place. Indeed, the concept of imposition is not so much a definition of power as of the *abuse* of power. So that where Rutter, for example, states that power refers to 'a difference in degree of personal and social freedom between two people that leads to one imposing his will on the other' (1990: 42), I would challenge this and prefer to stay with Weber – power may be imposed, but imposition is not the definition of power. This seems important if we are to acknowledge that power can be a positive force.

So, 'power over' is not a static commodity. It is ascribed as well as taken, and may vary from situation to situation. It seems that in therapy, however, many clients allow therapists to have power over them, some therapists exercise a power over their client, and some abuse power in relation to their clients. It seems that this is at least partly due to the structural aspects of the situation, and it may be helpful to look at the notions of authority, influence and force to enhance understanding here. They all carry a power dynamic, yet have differences which need to be overt. This may help to understand how it is that ascription of power to another, or abdication of self-empowerment, may occur, and, crucially, how it may be regained.

The ascription of authority is central here. Authority is assumed because of status or position, and is also ascribed for the same reason. One individual only ever has as much authority as is invested in him or her by self or others. Authority then has the notion of power invested in someone in order to fulfil particular objectives or tasks.

The grounds on which this may happen, which may then increase the potency of the person in whom it is invested, may be many, but I can think of no instance where it is not connected with knowledge (or assumed knowledge) of some kind. For example, age brings an authority in some cultures and societies, out of respect for the life experience of the older person. Professional status also brings or invests authority – teachers, doctors and lawyers are all invested with some authority – they are assumed to know what they are on about. This holds true in respect to therapists.

Where authority is abused within the therapeutic relationship, the abuse may be allowed because of a belief that the therapist knows best:

> He was a very brainy, forceful intellectual man, very caring, but I don't think now that he had any idea of professional boundaries. He was just playing the role of my father, and I thought well he knows what he's doing, maybe this is therapy.

The point is here that when we invest someone with knowledge, so do we invest that person with a certain authority, and thus that person becomes powerful. They know, we don't:

> That's the same tradition . . you can discuss questions of philosophy but you don't question what he asks you to do . . . in that role he knows best and he can ask anything of you virtually and its for your spiritual development he is asking you, but he won't necessarily tell you why he is asking you to do this or that.

> I thought well I'm working with a Jungian and I don't know how Jungians work so there was that whole thing of I don't know what to expect and I don't know what's okay and it's not anything I'm used to. So I went along and he could have said an awful lot of things or done an awful lot of things before I might have thought I know that Jungians don't really know that.

This belief in the authority of the therapist or of the trainer is one dimension which results in clients' self-doubt and in their complaisance.

Another aspect or manifestation of power is influence. Influence is the ability to change, modify or control people's behaviour or attitudes without the use of overt power or force. Therapists or trainers may be influential because of the authority they are perceived to have which is dependent on their perceived expertise.

Therefore, people look to them with respect and feel that they will learn from them:

> He was a Buddhist teacher . . so you have a relationship with your teacher and you don't ask questions of it. You have to take the word of the master really.

Even where an exploitative relationship entails negative or destructive influence, the client may feel that they have been positively influenced as well. Several people described an ambivalence about the whole situation and felt that they were helped as well as hindered. Two women identified very specific influences which they had gained from within an exploitative relationship which remained valuable to them.

> He encouraged me to always say what I felt and when I met up with him later that's what I did. Without him I wouldn't have had any talking cure. . . . He did do something helpful, instead of Occupational Therapy he encouraged me to do English A level, which really was good.

> One of the other things was that he introduced me to classical music. . . . I was learning things from him all the time.

Both women retrospectively thought that they should have had the attention and help without the sexual side, yet that these had been positive influences.

A final abuse of power which may be encountered in the therapeutic relationship is force. Force may be seen as operating along a continuum from coercion to physical brute force. They may go together.

> I had been working with him for eight months. He was sexualising everything I said and I challenged him about this repeatedly. It was difficult because he was my tutor and I was frightened of being thrown off the course. Eventually he became so frustrated that he lunged at me and grabbed me by both breasts and shook me for about thirty seconds.

In this case the direction of the therapy may be seen to be forced upon the client because of the power that the therapist had over her. This culminated in physical assault. This particular client made no complaint for fear of being thrown off the psychotherapy course she was studying, as the therapist was a key tutor.

We may see power then as entailing a set of relations between people, places and things. It is enabled and transmitted through language, ideas, images, practices and beliefs. For example, people may be powerful in relation to one another, institutions such as the Church, schools and the courts are powerful, buildings may be powerful in the evocations they produce. Thus we are talking about a dynamic force which may be used constructively or destructively depending on the context and on the value system of those involved.

Within therapeutic discourse, this dynamic sense of power has also been identified as being an energy force within the individual, and this is reflected in the notion of developing potential or potentiating the individual. This notion, heavily influenced by the psychology of Albert Maslow and of Carl Rogers, rests on the premise that people have a creative force within them which is often untapped. This is the energy which we use to exist, to learn and to interact with the world around us. As we go through life from infanthood to adulthood, so this energy is in play.

The faith of the counsellor in this context is that as adults we retain a reserve of power–energy force which is not always used, or is used in ways which fail to reach the full potential of the individual. This is a specifically value-oriented understanding, in the sense that there is a belief operating which states that the fully potentiated individual is a creative and constructive individual, in relation to him- or herself and to others.

Carl Rogers puts it this way:

> From the perspective of politics, power and control, person-centred therapy is based on a premise which at first seemed risky and uncertain: a view of man as at core a trustworthy organism. . . . I have recently described it as 'the gradually formed and tested hypothesis that the individual has within himself vast resources for self-understanding, for altering his self-concept, his attitudes, and his self-directed behaviour – and that these resources can be tapped if only a definable climate of facilitative psychological attitudes can be provided'. (1978: 7)

These resources, then, conceptualise the notion of potential and see the dynamism within this as inherent within each person.

Power in therapy

Power relates to therapy in more ways than within ideas of self and the human condition. Theories and ideologies carry their own power. For example, religious ideologies which incorporate the idea of the wrath of God can exert tremendous influence. Therapy has developed its own ideologies. The very fact that we now conceptualise experiences and behaviours as having a psychological basis is an ideology. Two hundred years ago this would not have been the case.

Ideologies are themselves then very powerful. Psychological theory has had tremendous impact on our way of life, starting really with Freud. Freudian theory, albeit vulgarised at times, has been used on a grand scale to influence our behaviour. The movement in the 1950s to keep women within the home tapped the whole notion of children having specific psychological needs which must be provided by their mothers. The seduction theory has made for all sorts of conceptualisations around the area of sexual abuse, so that there is still a strong belief in some schools of therapy that children routinely and subconsciously desire a sexual relationship with their parent of the opposite gender.

One of the more overt instances of the vulgarisation of theory with all its influence is told by a participant in my own research:

> One therapist (I never went back), he said, it's my penis you're after, you want to castrate me. I said, for Heaven's sake, stop this nonsense, I've come here as I'm having difficulty about relating to my daughter, I couldn't give a damn what you think about your penis. But that felt like a sexual abuse, it felt like pure Freudian theory. It was absolutely irrelevant to the help I needed. This was the first visit, I never went back.

Now clearly this was an extremely unskilled practitioner, and I would not like to attribute this method of working to Freud, but there is something very relevant in how we see here a practitioner completely hooked into a theoretical framework (incorrectly interpreted) which he then tries, unsuccessfully, to impose. We must acknowledge that any theory which is held to rigidly may have its own influence, first on the therapist who may try to fit everything into it, thus interpreting at the cost of listening, secondly upon the client, and thirdly upon particular groups of people who subscribe to it.

This may have been seen to happen with some feminist therapies over the last twenty years. The appropriation of objects–relation theory to a feminist bent became adopted not only by practitioners and therefore their clients, but informed much feminist theory and many women's groups. This resulted in a belief among those groups that mothers of daughters recreated their own problems within their daughters. This was first seen as an enabler to enhance understanding, but slowly became a straitjacket wherein women were seen to be responsible for all their daughters' ills.

Rigid belief or straitjacketing can itself be abusive or, at least, frightening for the client. One participant recalls:

> Then all of a sudden I thought, oh my God, you [the offending therapist] have been a transference for my father. . . . I realised my God, that's awful, that's terrible, really bad, so I was really fucked up by that and believed I must have wanted sex with my father.

This was particularly distressing since this particular client had been sexually abused by her father.

Psychotherapy has also become a powerful tool of diagnosis and of social control. Within the judicial process, those convicted of crime may be sent for a psychological or psychiatric assessment.

This may determine what kind of punishment or rehabilitation they receive. The word of the professional involved in this judgement becomes very powerful indeed, as does the profession itself.

Psychological theory has also been the justification for enforced regulation or incarceration of an individual. Mental Health Acts have empowered the state to designate people as mentally ill and to take whatever measures have been deemed necessary, sometimes using extreme force as with electroconvulsive therapy, restraint by straitjacket or drugs, or incarceration. On occasion psychotherapy has been imposed as a condition of punishment with or without the individual's consent. These measures have received a great deal of support and acceptance in society, as well as earning strong criticism from eminent psychiatrists such as Thomas Szasz, or the British anti-psychiatry movement in the 1960s. Organisations such as MIND have been set up to protect the rights of those designated mentally ill and to fight some of the practices outlined.

This all makes for a very powerful institutionalised system of help and control, and illustrates what a strong hold the ideology has or has had on modern Western society. In other words, the power of psychology has influenced us in terms of our everyday living as well as in our ideas of normality, deviance and retribution.

There is also the power of the process of therapy in the sense of what happens when, in our distress, we discover conditions of genuineness and warmth which may enable emotional discharge and the development of insight:

> At the time I was completely taken in, and I was very blocked, so when she finally succeeded in helping me get in touch with my feelings, I mean that too was very powerful.

The very act of experiencing something intense holds a power, a force, which is significant for the person in the client's chair. This may engender feelings towards the person who is perceived as helping with and then sharing in such an experience. Clients may express a feeling of the therapist being the only person who could be trusted at that time. Here it seems to me that the task of the therapist is to help the client develop trust in both him- or herself and other appropriate people, and to reduce the risk of dependency, by demystifying the process. The potential, of course, is for fostering the dependency and thus appropriating the invested power.

One participant was acutely aware of this potential.

> I know what a powerful position a [therapist] is in . . and it's really a terrible abuse to go beyond what you're supposed to do. . . . I'm not sure that all therapy isn't some kind of abuse. Now I'm doing co-counselling I can see what's wrong with any kind of therapy.

Because of such concerns about the power of therapy and its underlying ideology, there have been moves to 'outlaw' it as being *only* a means of social control and regulation. The most well known recent work on this subject is *Against Therapy* by Jeffrey Masson (1988). Masson argues that therapy is itself an abuse, that because of the power invested in it it can be little else. Therapists, he argues, necessarily become blind to any but their own theories, psychotherapy itself supports the political status quo, and therapists refuse to see abuse within the profession.

Masson details various abuses, and his argument deserves listening to. He can be criticised, however, for using material selectively, and for himself falling into the trap of not listening to clients of psychotherapy who feel that they have been helped. In other words, he analyses through his own ideologies. Perhaps the biggest flaw of this radical stance, namely that because psychotherapies can be abused they are always abusive, is a failure to look at the possibly beneficial *use* of power. Like Rutter, power is used by Masson only in the sense of its *abuse*. He sees it as necessarily constraining and controlling rather than enabling. This seems to be not only unconstructive but flawed. The possibility of power being an enabling force needs some mention and exploration.

Using power constructively

It must be acknowledged, then, that the therapist is in a powerful position. Also, we need to recognise in this context that sexuality and power have their own relationship. Because of how sexuality is constructed, power can elicit sexual response. Thus a charismatic therapist or trainer may provoke strong sexual attraction from the client or trainee. Moreover, within the therapeutic process, as we have already seen, conditions of warmth and genuineness may provoke a response which manifests as sexual whether or not this is really what the client wants, or whether it is the client's only means of obtaining attention and comfort.

For example, one participant states that he found emotional revelation extremely powerful:

> That was very powerful and then I did feel this enormous attraction, I did see her as this extraordinary woman.

The sharing of a powerful insight or emotional moment is an intimacy which must be acknowledged and treated with respect.

Conversely, it must be recognised that sexual attraction itself provokes a powerful response, which manifests both mentally and physiologically. This may sound like stating the obvious, namely that sexual attraction or lust is a powerful human experience. This has been recognised in all societies for all time. It is after all in one sense a basic drive to do with our survival. This is not to say that it is thus uncontrollable, as some myths would have it, or that it can only take direction. It would simply be dishonest to underestimate the impact that sexual feelings can have at times.

In suggesting that power is a dynamic force, it does not detract from the possibility that this can be an energetic force within the individual. Hence such terms as empowerment or disempowerment. Using one's own power, tapping into both dynamic energy and knowledge is not only possible but often central to learning and personal development.

Two approaches may be used to illustrate how the potency of therapy can be used without disempowering or disabling the client. One focuses on the power of transference within the therapeutic relationship, whereas the other may be seen as illustrating empowerment of the client as the central focus of a problem-solving approach to counselling.

Within psychodynamic theory, the relationship between the therapist and client is seen as the central tool and any feelings which arise within it are used as part of the therapy. This must be treated with caution, as to solicit or elicit particular feelings to fit into a predetermined model may be disabling. Nevertheless, the principle of working with whatever feelings do arise is a valid and constructive one when used with respect. One of the participants in my research who had been abused outside and inside the therapeutic relationship found enormous empowerment in this approach. She approached another male therapist in the belief that it was important to confront her own issues of sexuality. She took her own power into the situation by immediately telling him of the previous abuse and stating that this must not happen again.

With the new therapist, she felt sexual arousal at times and declared this. He allowed this and they explored what need she was ultimately expressing, which seemed to be the need to be held. She declared any point at which she felt sexually aroused, which she felt confident, because of clear contracting, that he would not act on. At one point he felt sexually attracted or aroused and declared this with the demonstration that he would not act on his own feeling. Together they worked to a greater understanding of her needs and she managed to break an old pattern of using sex to obtain affection. His precise and clear keeping of boundaries were crucial, and the experience was immensely liberating for her. Moreover, she developed an insightful understanding to her that she was working with transference feelings to do with her parents, and understood that she was not attracted to the male therapist himself.

The other way of working which hinges on the concept of power as a driving force in individual development is to approach the therapeutic goal from the problem-solving end of the spectrum. This way of working is best illustrated by Egan (1990) and builds on the philosophical foundations of Carl Rogers. Such an approach is fuelled by conditions of respect, empathy and genuineness. In other words, the worker must be for the client and be working towards helping the client to develop his or her own *potential* as an equal human being.

A three-stage model of working with sexual abuse and sexuality appears in Chapter 8. The three stages recognise that within counselling the client may need to explore past events in relation to the present and the future, and be helped to set realistic goals which are within the client's value system. All of this needs to be clearly contracted and operates within defined boundaries.

Where the model differs from others is in its recognition that issues of sexuality and power for the worker may be present throughout the counselling process. If the worker is faced squarely with this reality from the outset, then they are more likely to address the issues which may lead to control or exploitative practice. This is dealt with in more detail in the chapter on practical recommendations (see Chapter 8).

Some general principles apply to all counselling. The genuine acceptance of another's feelings may also help that person to find his or her own empowerment. Society teaches that it is undesirable to feel strong emotions of anger or sadness, and sometimes individuals use a tremendous amount of energy in suppressing such feelings. Respectful empathic response is a powerful tool in enabling the expression of such feelings. The realisation from the client that this is acceptable can be tremendously empowering and aid self-acceptance. Self-acceptance releases energy that has previously been used in turmoil.

Reflecting people's strengths is important in therapy. This is particularly advocated in problem-solving counselling approaches, and other therapies might use similar techniques. The temptation with many helpers is to collude with the difficulties or distress of the client. It can be enormously empowering to reflect what strengths and abilities the client has and to build on these. This is only possible when the therapist does not fall into the trap of seeing the client as helpless. Every voluntary client has at the very least a motivation to change whatever is currently difficult, and has found some strategies to get this far, whether or not those strategies are now redundant. To recognise this is to recognise that each individual does have his or her own power, but that sometimes help is needed in tapping into it.

Skilled challenging is also a respectful acknowledgement and enhancer of the client's potential. Human beings can be very good at disabling themselves, and sometimes reflection of inconsistencies, exaggerations and discrepancies can help to reframe the problem under review.

The list could go on, and there are many ways in which therapists of different kinds can work in a way which aids empowerment. It is not that they have the power to give to clients, rather the task is to stimulate the clients' release of their own power. To some extent, this is acknowledging a belief system that human beings have potential and that within this is the possibility of self-enhancement.

The work of Gerard Egan (see, for example, Egan, 1973, 1990) encapsulates this perspective when he emphasises that effective helping is an educational process. The client is encouraged and aided to develop personal insights through a process of understanding and which then equips the client with additional tools and skills with which to live life more effectively. Although Egan's model is often vulgarised, I would argue that used skilfully it makes for therapeutic interventions which tap into the power, or the energy, that the client is using in living ineffectively. This has to be a positive and constructive act.

Moreover, the more the client understands the process, the less potential there exists for exploitation. The research which informs this book suggests that ignorance on the part of the client fuelled the capacity of the therapist to exploit, and delayed the ability in the client to resist. It seems logical that the less mystery the better.

Conclusions

It seems that the abuse of power is possible in therapy for several reasons. The therapist is invested with authority and is influential. On occasion the therapist can use force to obtain desired outcomes.

The very theory and practice of therapy enables this power to be ascribed. Psychological theories exist in an ideological framework which has had tremendous impact on Western twentieth-century thought, both in everyday life practices and in the area of social control. They can be tremendously powerful to both the therapist and the client.

Awareness of the possibilities of abuse of this inherent power has led to a backlash which sees all therapy as abusive. However, little consideration has been given to the constructive use of power. This seems to be because the term power is not addressed fully but confused with abuse of power. In examining the constructive potentials, we see that therapy can be empowering in certain circumstances. Therapists need to treat their clients and their work with respect and to engender an educative process within the clients where understanding is aided, thus reducing the risk of exploitation.

PART TWO PRACTICAL IMPLICATIONS FOR COUNSELLING AND THERAPY

7

ETHICAL DIMENSIONS TO THE PROBLEM

I would have expected him to be more professional and to behave in an ethical manner.

When we talk about behaving unethically, we perhaps take for granted that we share a common understanding of what constitutes ethical behaviour. This may not always be the case, however, and it is worth exploring what we understand the concept to mean. It will be helpful to look at a variety of scenarios to explore some of the possible dilemmas which may arise under the umbrella of ethics. This may help us formulate some of the principles of good practice.

Conceptualising

It is perhaps useful to make a general distinction between values, ethics and morality. All are related and yet may be seen as discrete categories. A common distinction to be made is that *morality* refers to that which is right or wrong, *ethics* may be seen as the code of morals operated by an individual, group or profession, and *values* may be seen as reflecting the system by which individuals subjectively rank what is 'good' or 'bad'. So for example, it may be acceptable within a value system to be married rather than cohabiting, because this is seen as ethically correct for a particular ethnic group and reflects a moral stance of the society in which it operates.

In a recent work on legal and ethical dilemmas within psychotherapy, Austin et al. make a similar threefold distinction between morals, ethics and values. Drawing on the philosophical tradition, they suggest that values refer to that which we deem to be good and desirable, that ethics refer to that which we think is right and ought to be done, whereas morality refers to a code of practice which relates to a community standard, and which is evaluative and holds a notion of judgement (1990: 241). All three categories are culturally and historically specific.

Within this, then, we can see that ethics are implicitly normative, and hold something of the categorical imperative, the *should* of the specific situation. They are derived from and informed by values. The normative function may be seen in action when it comes to enforcing standards within counselling and therapeutic practice, through supervision or through the design and implementation of training programmes, and through the accreditation process of professional bodies.

Ethical codes and the professions

This leads us on to the idea of professional bodies having codes of ethics and why they do. The most well known example of an ethical code with which we are familiar in the West is the Hippocratic oath, which states that:

> I swear by Apollo the physician and by Aesculapius to keep the following oath: I will prescribe for the good of my patients and never do harm to anyone. In every house where I come I will enter only for the good of my patients, keeping myself far from all intentional ill-doing and all seduction, and especially from the pleasures of love with women or men, be they free or slaves.

This principle has been both adapted and adopted by the psychological world, although we may see a different rationale. On the one hand we can see that the development of psychotherapy owes much to the development of psychiatry, which is closely linked to the medical world and its (generally) recognised scientific status. On the other hand, the subject matter is less tangible. Perhaps one of the most important aspects of any rationale is the understanding of the power and intensity of the therapeutic relationship. We are indebted to Freud for such recognition which is couched in terms of transference. I would take the idea wider and highlight three particular points which are crucial to this discussion.

The first is the ascription of authority to the therapist by both client and by society. It is also claimed through the seeking of professional and/or accredited status. As the demand for account-ability increases, there is a corresponding increase in the recognition that the therapeutic relationship has an inherent duality which is both its justification, or strength, and its weakness:

> The duality inheres in the concept of authority . . . it refers to an individual who is a specialist in his or her field and is entitled to credit or acceptance on this basis; in another sense, it refers to power that requires submission. (Karasu, 1980: 1050)

In other words, it is the concept of authority which makes the therapist creditworthy:

> I couldn't very easily challenge what he was doing. I knew he was a member of the X institute and I assumed that he was supervised.
>
> I thought well she's a professional, with a high degree of professional awareness, with a very good practice, and teaching experience and all that, she's involved in training, supervision, on an international basis.

For therapy to work, the client has to be able to assume that the therapist is competent.

There is also the notion, however, that to trust someone, based on perceived creditworthiness, involves some relinquishing of power:

> In order to work through these issues, I had to trust him and I think I had this sort of quite erroneous notion that I had to allow him power in order to do that.

So the potential to make it work is the same potential which enables abusive or exploitative practice. This is what is meant by the inherent duality. Ethical codes recognise this and demand from the professional an adherence to a high standard of morality. Shapiro (1987) recognises that this standard is perhaps higher than is prevalent in the wider community. This may of course be an unattainable ideal.

Correspondingly, the second point about the power and intensity of the relationship is the vulnerability of the client. While not wishing to see the client as helpless or passive, it must be recognised that there may be doubts about the ability of the person in the client's shoes to give informed consent, or to be able to discern whether an activity or suggestion is going to be beneficial. In my research I was struck by how many participants re-evaluated their experiences which they had allowed at moments of vulnerability, and by the ambivalent responses they had to what took place within the sessions:

> I wanted that sort of contact . . . I was pretty naive . . . I knew that he shouldn't be doing what he was doing.
>
> I was getting very distressed . . . I was in a therapeutic state.

The recognition of vulnerability and the possibility of submissive behaviour is an important part of the rationale for ethical codes.

The third and final point on the rationale of the ethical stance is the recognition that one aspect of what therapy is about is the confession and exploration of the client's inner thoughts and feelings. I would distinguish here between the extremes of pure psychoanalysis and problem-solving counselling models, but it seems that within the general notion of therapy, self-exploration is widely encouraged and accepted as part of the process.

It is, then, not uncommon for some exploration of the client's sexual world to be a part of the process. It is also widely believed and practised that the interpersonal relationship between therapist and client is at least important to the process, and sometimes one of the tools. Whether we agree with this perspective or not, it can be seen that these factors give therapists privileged access to intimate knowledge of the client which they might react to personally, whether with stimulation, disgust, ease or difficulty. One participant in my research commented:

> He opened up the sexual side of me then didn't know how to deal with it.

Several participants bemoaned a denial of sexual dynamics on the part of the therapist.

As I suggested in Chapter 1, such rationales and the presence of ethical codes shows an acceptance that unethical practice exists. In relation to sexual intimacies, Ray Hays makes the same point:

> The fact that such sexual contact is specifically proscribed for the two major [US] mental health professions does not prevent that activity from occurring. In fact, if such contact did not exist the proscription would seem unnecessary. (1980: 1247)

Austin et al. (1990) elucidate six functions of ethical codes:

1 To bestow prestige upon the profession.
2 To provide guidelines which provide a focus of consensus over complex issues.
3 To define the boundaries of responsibility to the client, the profession and to society, (which supposedly provides a protective function for all parties).
4 To offer autonomy to the organisation to be self-regulating and therefore dependent on its own integrity.
5 For the purpose of evaluation, as through supervision and training programmes.
6 For normative development through the same means.

If we accept these functions, we can see that the fourth is immediately contentious. If an organisation is self-regulated, then it is immediately open to both the risk and the accusation of being self-serving as its primary value. It is an accusation we have seen the police force faced with time and time again when it launches an internal inquiry. The public sees a closing of ranks, whether or not this is actually operating.

Once a code of ethics is in place, it becomes enforceable by an internal body who will be *seen* as partisan, and who may *be* partisan. One potential participant in my research decided against participation because she felt that the network was contaminated, in that she perceived that the emphasis would be on organisational protection, or that members of the ethics committee might be open to question. This apprehension was echoed by other participants who felt unable to use the ethical committees of organisations involved as they anticipated finding them to be both sexist and self-protective. One participant complained to her governing body about an assault only to find that the therapist involved was on that very committee. The point is that clients have no guarantee of objectivity in this situation.

Two illustrations might make the point more graphically, and help to draw out the subtleties of it. One involved a woman, Penny (pseudonym), who had made a complaint to the Health Authority about her experience of inappropriate and offensive behaviour by a clinical psychologist. She was granted a meeting with the psychologist in the presence of an arbitrator and a person of her choice. The arbitrator was the manager of the Mental Health Services.

Penny invited me to accompany her as she felt that my interest and research orientation was validating to her. The purpose of the meeting was twofold for her. First, she wanted to feel that her perspective was being both listened to and taken seriously, and secondly, she sought an apology which illustrated this.

She had from the outset suspected that the manager would be biased, and expressed reservations about the meeting place, which was to be the hospital where she had been a patient. In other words, the very context of the meeting, in terms of place and participants, felt biased and unsafe.

When we arrived at the hospital, we were shown into the patients' waiting room and were called ten minutes later than scheduled. When we were shown into the meeting room, the manager and the psychologist were already there. For Penny, this suggested complicity and heightened her anxiety level.

During the course of the meeting, I was struck particularly by three points which I felt were collusive with the self-protective angle. The first was that the psychologist refused to answer questions on the content of the clinical session under question on the grounds of confidentiality. The questions pertained to the intention of the interventions which the client was objecting to. This seemed extraordinary to my understanding of confidentiality, which incorporates the notion that its existence is for the client's benefit. Thus the client may divulge the content of any therapeutic session whereas a practitioner may not. Should a client ask that confidentiality be waived, stating that it is not required in a particular circumstance, then this protective function ceases to be. Thus the private becomes secretive, and for the protection of the worker.

The second point involved the psychologist making it very clear to the client that he was hurt by her suggestions, particularly 'after all I've done for you'. The third point involved my presence in the complaints process. Penny had specifically invited me to ask any questions I would like to, and the questions I asked pertained specifically to the points above. At this stage the psychologist asked me my job and my interest. From the moment of my answering this question, the climate visibly changed. An apology was indeed forthcoming, although much of the ensuing discussion had involved more eye contact with me than with Penny.

I was struck by how the mental health manager failed to facilitate the strong emotions involved in this process. It is my belief in fact that she was unsure how to, and that she was unpractised in this kind of complaint. There seemed to be more a lack of awareness and of experience than intentional neglect. Also, I have no doubt that the psychologist's responses reflected a position of vulnerability, perhaps reflecting his own lack of support.

In both manner and structure, however, this meeting did not hold any promise for the client of fair and unbiased arbitration. When we left, again the two Health Authority workers remained in the room, with Penny feeling that there was a collusion of protection. I understand that this particular health authority has now negotiated independent arbitration for any future such meetings.

For Penny, the story did not end there. She still felt cheated of both real acknowledgement and of adequate treatment, a view which was shared by law centre workers who subsequently became involved. She was left with no doubt that there were definite sides being taken. In a personal letter to me sometime after, Penny wrote;

> I'm gradually getting my faculties back, due to the strengths coming from my determination that 'they' did not succeed in squashing me out of sight.

This view of them and us indicates that whatever the interests of a professional grouping, they may be seen to be different to that of the client group.

Another participant had made a complaint to a different Health Authority about the treatment she had received from a Community

Psychiatric Nurse. The case is complex, but for this client it hinges around failure to work with strong sexual and affectionate feelings, inadequate termination of therapy, and dismissal of complaint. Feeling that she was getting nowhere at the hospital concerned, she wrote to the Health Service Commissioner. It is appropriate to quote at length from his reply;

> I cannot investigate action taken in connection with the diagnosis of illness or the care or treatment of a patient if, in my opinion, it was taken solely in consequence of the exercise of clinical judgement. In my view the essence of your complaint, and your major grievances, either relate directly to the manner in which Mr [X] and his successors provided a service to you, or stem from the relationships which developed between you and the therapists. Both aspects are, in my opinion, inextricably bound up with the clinical judgement of the staff in question and, for that reason, I have concluded that I cannot investigate them.

Clinical judgement may become a screen which debars acknowledgement of clumsy or inappropriate manner and behaviour, and which may influence questions of ethical conduct. While organisations and professions are self-regulating, there is no doubt that they will continue to be seen at times as putting their own interests first, whether or not this is the case. This will be true for both statutory and independent organisations.

Codes of ethics

The recently revised edition of the codes of ethics and practice for the British Association for Counselling (BAC) is at pains to point out that it can only offer guidelines, a frame of reference, and this view seems to me to be realistic. We know that sometimes codes of ethics may contravene other codes, such as that of confidentiality, or of the law. Although operating some consensus for the profession, we must also acknowledge that codes of ethics may pose contradictions for members of that profession, or for organisations in which they work. It will be useful to look at some of the major British codes of ethics with examples of what people in this research felt contravened them.

Counsellor–client relationship

The BAC *Code of Ethics and Practice for Counsellors* has undergone extensive revision over the last two years. The 1984 code states that

> Engaging in sexual activity with a client while also engaging in a therapeutic relationship is unethical.

This provides a very clear prohibition. The revised version (1990: 2.7) makes a more general ethical statement, namely that 'counselling is a non-exploitative activity'. This is one of four statements which purport to outline the fundamental values and general principles of the profession, and expansion and detail is provided in the accompanying code of practice. The specifically relevant points here are made in items 2.2.5 and 2.2.6 of this latter code.

> 2.2.5. Counsellors are responsible for setting and monitoring boundaries between the counselling relationship and any other kind of relationship, and making this explicit to the client.

> 2.2.6. Counsellors must not exploit their clients financially, sexually, emotionally or in any other way. Engaging in sexual activity with the client is unethical. (BAC *Code of Ethics and Practice*, 1990)

As I have argued elsewhere (Russell, 1990), this seems to be a progression in terms of recognising sexual exploitation as a question of boundary breaking, and as one of a number of forms of exploitation. I feel also that the definitive final statement helps to relate our practice to a wider morality.

In terms of practice, this code goes slightly further than most by stating that not only are counsellors responsible for boundary setting, but also for *making this explicit to the client*. This simple but central requirement, if followed, helps to at least reduce the possibilities of misunderstandings or lack of clarity for the client. My personal preference is to see the ethical limitations of the relationship between therapists and clients explicated in the contract at the very outset. More will be said on this in Chapter 8.

The code of conduct for the British Psychological Society states that members:

> shall . . . not exploit the special relationship of trust and confidence that can exist in professional practice to further the gratification of their personal desires. (1985: 5.2)

This is helpful in recognising some of the particular qualities of the therapeutic relationship which potentiate exploitation. Trust, for example, is one of the central components. Many clients conceptu- . alise such exploitation as a betrayal of trust:

> I felt that he had completely betrayed my trust. I see this as a gross violation of trust.

The clause is also helpful in recognising that the gain in potential exploitation for the therapist is self-gratification.

The Association of Sexual and Marital Therapists' code of ethics states that:

The personal dignity of clients is to be recognised at all times. The therapist must always act according to his or her professional judgement in the client's best interest. Care must be exercised by the therapist not to abuse the client–therapist relationship financially, sexually or in any other way. (1986: 3)

They explicate in the code of practice that:

It is not acceptable for a therapist to have a sexual relationship with anyone who is her or his own client. (ibid.: 4.2)

The Institute of Humanistic and Traditional Psychotherapies states that:

The professional relationship precludes sexual involvement with clients. (1989: 2)

The Gestalt Psychotherapy Training Institute (UK) is more fulsome:

The relationship between the Gestalt psychotherapist and his or her client is obviously fundamental to the therapy. Therapists need to recognise the power and influence which the contract of psychotherapy gives them, and the likelihood of their being recipients of numerous projections. They should not permit their professional skills to be used in a way to manipulate people to the benefit of other persons or organisations. Gestalt psychotherapists must not exploit their clients financially, sexually or emotionally (sexual intercourse with a client is regarded as exploitation). (1988: 3)

This is helpful in its overt mentions of power, influence, and the directive not to exploit. It is interesting that sexual intercourse is specifically mentioned, for while this in some ways delineates the behaviour too narrowly, it is also helpful in making a clear and specific prohibition.

The Institute of Psychotherapy and Social Studies requires that:

Practitioners recognise the importance of a good working relationship for effective therapy or tuition, and are cognizant of the power and influence they have. Professional relationships exclude abuse or exploitation – financial, sexual, emotional, physical or whatever. (1989: 7)

This locates sexual exploitation firmly within the context of abuse of influence or power. It also likens the therapist–client relationship to that of tutor–student (this becomes relevant in the following section).

A final example is from the code of ethics of the National Register of Hypnotherapists and Psychotherapists, which declares that:

Therapists do not exploit their clients financially, sexually or emotionally. If a sexual or financial relationship (other than the payment of legitimate fees) develops between therapist and client (or a member of the client's immediate family) the therapist should immediately cease to accept fees, and should transfer the client to another therapist as soon as possible. (1989: 7)

This adds a new dimension to the problem – is it acceptable to terminate therapy in deference to the sexual relationship which has developed? – that is to say, is it acceptable to say 'we're attracted to each other so let's just stop the therapy'? Experience suggests that this is not helpful as the therapist remains in role to some extent, as might the client. It gives no space for the discovery of whether this is a real and valid attraction between two mature adults or whether it is of an idealising or exploitative nature.

On the other hand, if the attraction is so strong that it cannot be worked with, it is appropriate to refer to another therapist. The question then remains whether the original attraction can be pursued without violating ethical codes. Many relationships develop between people who have unequal power bases, and one argument is that choice should not be denied. Yet it is clear that in subscribing to a professional ethical code, the therapist must show that while being human, he or she behaves in a way which is as morally unreprehensible as possible. This would entail acknowledgement that the situation and role differential may have influenced attraction, and therefore the practitioner must be prepared to leave a useful time gap before the client is allowed to make contact socially. It seems important that the initiative should be with the client, as it gives the client the prerogative of changing his or her mind and not feeling pressured, and allows the client to gain control of the situation. A minimum time gap of six months seems to me to be reasonable.[1] This gives some time for cooling off and re-evaluation of the feelings and issues which are pertinent to the situation.

Three participants in my research spring to mind here. In one case, a relationship evolved from tutor–trainee to counsellor–client to lovers. Here the woman involved felt in retrospect that the behaviour was totally wrong, and was able to tell the man concerned at a later date that:

I'm really really angry with you . . . it's all been phoney, it's not real . . . there's no way that you should have abused the situation, abused . . . I know I was seductive, I know what state I was in, mentally I was just so far regressed into my child that I was a sitting duck.

Another participant, male, had a sexual relationship with his ex-therapist after some time had elapsed, yet still felt that:

It was a gross betrayal of trust. . . . I had this enormous transference to her . . . it was deeply incestuous.

Clearly for these participants, the termination of the therapy did not justify the relationship. For a third participant, there was a day between therapy session and sexual encounter. This was in a context where other boundaries had been broken, and was experienced as highly destructive.

This selection of codes, then, is not intended as a complete list but intended to raise some of the ethical issues and dilemmas which are pertinent to ethical codes of practice for the counsellor–client relationship.

Trainer–trainee relationship

What of the trainer–trainee relationship – how ethical is it for this to become sexual? The BAC *Code of Ethics and Practice for Trainers* states that:

> Trainers are responsible for setting and monitoring the boundaries between working relationships and friendships or other relationships . . . and should not engage in sexual activity with their trainees whilst also engaging in a training relationship. (1985: 1.5)

Five participants in my research pointed up this situation. Jay (pseudonym) wrote to me having just left a counselling course:

> I have left because the course leader manipulated me (I felt) into a sexual situation with him. It has caused me a few problems.

This woman was left feeling tremendously angry and with a feeling of having her trust betrayed. In working within an experiential group facilitated by the tutor, she had looked at some sexual issues occasioned by the break-up of a long-term relationship. The tutor and herself later entered a sexual relationship. Jay writes:

> I am angry because I feel that I have been manipulated . . . one of my difficulties was sexual frustration . . . this was not an invitation to sex from [X] or anyone else . . . I am angry because I have had to scrutinise my own behaviour and ask myself whether I invited this. I have to say I feel I did not *but even if I had been overtly seductive . . . I feel that he should have been sufficiently professional to have dealt with this in the group and personal boundaries would not have been breached.* (emphasis in original)

She goes on to say how isolated she now felt as she was unable to use the group forum for personal exploration. She did in fact leave the course.

Another woman I interviewed, Alice (pseudonym), described her relationship with her course tutor who offered her counselling and subsequently became her lover. The counselling was offered in response to her request for help when she was extremely distressed over her father, who had sexually abused her. Within the counselling, she comments:

> He'd hold my hand, he'd be quite comforting . . . he seemed quite
> moved by some of the things I was telling him, I felt he was genuinely
> concerned.

He later suggested that she was seductive, and that this may have been one of her problems.

It seemed significant to Alice that much of the counselling was about her sexuality, and the difficulty that she had in relating to men in any other way than sexually. While still having counselling, she met her tutor/counsellor at a party and invited him to bed. They then began an affair which lasted for some time. While she is clear that she was proactive in the situation, she feels strongly that the tutor should have been able to keep his boundaries from the beginning. I understand that the course in question has now made a policy that tutors should not counsel students.

Two other people talked about this situation from the perspective of being on a course where a tutor had a sexual relationship with another member of the group. Esme (pseudonym) made the observation that selected students would be invited to tutors' houses socially, and that this made for a sort of exclusive group 'which I think was bad'. Her course had a largely experiential component wherein tutors would facilitate a 'sort of therapy group'. She felt that the facilitators here should have a sort of modelling role for the students:

> I think the way the boundaries were badly broken in our year was bad
> modelling, and I used to think that there wasn't enough emphasis on how
> important boundaries really are in counselling.

Esme identified two areas of effect which the relationship had on her. One was to pose a dilemma of whether or not she should tell the course director.

> I felt a lot of loyalty to the person who told me about this and therefore
> whilst I thought it was extremely unethical it put me in some difficulty as
> . . . to whether I should actually tell the course director she felt that she
> would be blamed . . . because of her inexperience in therapy . . . she
> couldn't be expected to know what the rules were but he was an
> experienced counsellor and a tutor on a course who should have the
> boundary and should be modelling the boundaries.

The other major effect was to destroy any trust that the students had in the tutor. They had often felt that he was covertly discussing his own material when posing the ethical dilemma of the counsellor attracted to the client. The affair consolidated the sense of unease that they had.

Jon (pseudonym) had been a participant on a recognised training course where one of the tutors (male) had a sexual relationship with a participant (female). The student told her support group in confidence, which was later to pose problems. The matter came to a head when the student's husband discovered the affair and informed the course director.

Jon felt that the consequences entailed two main feelings. One was an 'enormous betrayal of trust', and the other was extreme anger about how a residential week was then spent having to deal with the issues arising. This was exacerbated by the course director's refusal to accept responsibility for taking disciplinary action:

> He had fucked up that week which was an important residential week for us on a training programme, and the staff went into total disarray because they all felt betrayed by him. . . . It [the course] was person-centred, they wouldn't take responsibility.

Since then, because of the difficulties and resentment caused by the situation, the tutor in question has in fact resigned, some two years after the event.

Jon felt very strongly about the adverse effect of the whole episode:

> One of the things that concerned me most was kicking up a stink about it, making it public that this went on on my programme. I feel there is a sort of vicarious guilt here. [People might say] oh you are on the course that had the course tutor shagging his student, and like I am responsible. I feel I would get the blame and I didn't want to throw down two and a half years of hard work.

So not to tell presents problems of collusion, whereas telling presents a sort of stigmatised situation, where the students feel that if the course is brought into disrepute, their own reputation will be harmed.

I asked Jon in the course of the interview what he might like to see in place which would have helped the situation. He feels that a code of ethics from the governing body which explicitly prohibits such sexual contact, coupled with guidelines about making a complaint, would be helpful. He also felt that explicit contracting between trainer and trainees that there will be no sexual contact would be useful 'because that way people would feel safe'. In other words, there would be no room for ambiguity.

Jon expressed reservations about whether there should *never* be a relationship between tutor and student, where all concerned are mature. The problem seems to be firstly to distinguish between a 'real' relationship and a vicarious/opportunistic one. It would seem that where attraction is high, it is appropriate to deal with this in a supported, supervised manner, rather than in a covert, secretive or furtive way.

In my own experience, I have tutored with a co-tutor and student who had a pre-existing relationship. Our roles were negotiated openly, the group were aware of the situation, appropriate steps were taken to ensure that subjectivity did not affect marking, with the cooperation of the external examiner, and the process appeared to be manageable for all concerned.

Having said that, it was not without its difficult points, which were different for them both. From the tutor's perspective, the only possible justification for this situation was that the personal relationship pre-dated the tutorial relationship. Within this, the clear negotiations which included the other tutor, and which included making the relationship explicit to the group from the beginning helped with the management. A supportive and clear co-working relationship was helpful here. He felt it encumbent upon himself and his partner to model very clear boundaries, and felt that this was one of the pluses, in as much as this was an opportunity for them to practice a process which would remain important to their professional and personal relationship.

He felt at times that he was more cautious about sharing personal information and experience than he might otherwise have been, and feels that he was more constrained than his partner in this respect. This seemed appropriate as she was the student on the course. In sum, his attitude was that:

> It is a complication to be avoided if possible, but it is manageable if there is a very good working relationship between the tutors and the relationship is fairly robust and has clear boundaries. It does test the relationship.

From the student's perspective, there were apprehensions how she would be perceived by the other participants, wanting to be seen as a person in her own right and wanting to be trusted that she could observe the confidentiality ground rules. She felt enormous relief when the relationship was disclosed, and in the disclosure felt that this seemed to facilitate other group members' sharing of difficult boundary situations. Nevertheless, she remained nervous for the first term and felt that it was 'definitely baggage'.

On the whole, she felt able to share as openly as she wanted to although one incident remained undisclosed as it was intimately concerned with her partner. She made a point of not spending time with tutors at breaks and lunch and felt that some of the banter concerning their relationship was quite light and enabling. One difficulty was if they had had a disagreement outside the course, she felt it difficult to take an opportunity to regain intimacy and therefore had to work with the unresolved situation.

It would be interesting to know how this affected the group. It seemed at the end of the course that people had been slightly daunted by the added dynamic, but in fact over time had worked with it and felt very comfortable. In some way perhaps it gave them another insight into their tutor. My own perception and understanding of feedback leads me to believe that this was one factor in an open, committed and constructive learning experience.

One area which remains unclear is whether or not it would be ethical for a tutor and trainee to begin a sexual relationship after a course has finished and if so, what length of time should lapse before it would be appropriate to do so. There will always be a sense of arbitrariness in any time which is suggested, but six months would seem to be a reasonable guideline, as this gives both parties time to develop a wider perspective. It would at least raise the issue and provide some time for both parties to consider whether it is appropriate and for the tutor to address the issue within supervision and within any other support network. Less seems to be unrealistic, whereas longer may deny two adults the possibility of an equal and fulfilling relationship.

Supervisor–supervisee relationship

There is also the question of the supervisor–supervisee relationship. The BAC code of ethics states that:

> 2.3. Supervisors and counsellors are both responsible for setting and maintaining clear boundaries between working relationships and friendships or other relationships.

During this research, I came across no incidences of reported abuse. There were one or two situations however which are pertinent.

One woman I know is a worker for a voluntary organisation which deals primarily with sexual abuse. In the course of her supervision, she disclosed and worked through some personal material which seemed appropriate at the time. She found the session very useful. At the end of what she saw as a very helpful process, she was taken aback at the supervisor's suggestion that they should hug, yet she found herself complaisant while uncomfortable. She was not suggesting that this was sexually abusive, more that it was disempowering. It had not occurred before, and seemed directly relevant to the fact that she had disclosed intimate material. She felt patronised by the hug, despite having a great respect for the worker involved. It felt inappropriate that the suggestion should come from the supervisor. What surprised her most was how she acquiesced against her gut feeling.

A male colleague now makes it explicit in his contracting that there will be no sexual relationship between himself and the supervisee as the professional relationship is agreed. He tells me that one or two of his supervisees have looked a little surprised at the very suggestion, but that at least one woman has subsequently expressed how pleased she is that this was made explicit as she became attracted to him over the months.

One other situation was discussed with me which is relevant. A female counsellor and her client became aware of a strong attraction. They terminated the counselling contract in a manner which seemed appropriate to both women, acknowledging the issues and making plans for further counselling for the client. They then negotiated a time span after which the client would contact the counsellor if she still wished to.

The counsellor took this to supervision to ensure, as she thought, that her actions were appropriate and ethical. Her supervisor was not satisfied and reported her to the appropriate governing body. For the counsellor, this was perceived as a betrayal of trust and she commented that it would have been better not to go to supervision with this issue at all. This perhaps highlights the need for clear contracting, and for open discussion and consideration of the possibilities of sexual attraction.

Ethical committees

Most professional bodies which carry a code of ethics also have an ethics committee in place to both consider and inform standards of practice, and to deal with complaints from the client group. Procedure will differ between organisations. It is not appropriate here to go into all the different procedures and details, but I would like to draw out one or two points to highlight some of the limitations of ethics committees.

The first point is that many clients are not aware of whether or not their therapist is a member of a particular professional organisation. In my research, only three participants said that they knew this information. They then may not know how to approach the ethics committee – what is the procedure for clients?

Even if they do have this information, two possible problems may ensue. One is not having the courage, insight or ability to make an approach, and the second is in not trusting the organisation to be objective, fair or believing, a point made earlier when I referred to 'contaminated networks'. Some examples might help to clarify this.

One participant was himself an experienced therapist and knew of the existence of ethical committees and of the complaints procedure. He felt, however, that he was unable to use them:

> I don't think there's any way . . . I don't think it's a problem that any patient or client should ever have to deal with. I just don't think you're in the right [emotional] place.

Many participants echoed this. One woman, concerned to make a complaint by letter, is still hesitant:

> My fears about writing were, and I don't know how ungrounded they were, my big fear was that they would say Oh God, another hysterical woman, and bin it.

Another participant had rung up a professional organisation to ask how she would go about making a complaint and was put off by the telephone response, in which she was informed that this was a very serious step, and asked if she was sure of her facts. This seemed disabling to her at the time, and she would have welcomed the opportunity for informal discussion.

Some participants simply did not trust the organisation to be sympathetic, feeling that they were too involved to be impartial. They also expressed concern about the formality of the procedure and apprehensions about how long it may take.

Fears seem not to be totally ungrounded. One woman went through a complicated process which ended in frustration and the sense that she was up against a brick wall. As a student on a psychodynamic therapy course, she had been in personal therapy for nine months when her therapist sexually assaulted her. This seemed to be a climax to a series of inappropriate verbal interventions in which she experienced him 'sexualising' everything. Under pressure, she agreed not to disclose the assault, as the situation was complicated by the therapist also being a tutor on the course. The agreement not to disclose seemed to be underpinned by threat and apprehension of her not passing the course. He later abused her again. Hostilities ensued between them, and she did eventually report what had happened. The next difficulty was that the tutor involved was on the ethics committee. Eventually the committee met without the student present and asked her to leave the course.

> I couldn't complain because the future of my career was at stake. . . . When I did, I couldn't get heard and was made to feel like a criminal. He used authority without responsibility. I'm still boiling about the whole thing.

This echoes the American experience, where this particular problem has been acknowledged openly for much longer than in

Britain. The establishment of ethics committees is one of the favoured options for 'remedy'. However, they are perceived to have a limited success. Gartrell et al. (1987) report that only 23 per cent of cases which are reported to the American Psychiatric Association, for example, are proved. They recount that one woman, herself a psychiatrist, made a complaint which took four years to reach conclusion, only to have the perceived abuse dismissed as insignificant. They conclude, as experienced therapists and researchers in this area, that 'I would never refer a patient of mine to the ethics committee' (Gartrell et al., 1987: 1130).

We could learn a lot from the procedures which seem *not* to be working with these committees in the United States, while recognising that there will always be problems with the self-regulating nature of the profession.

Ethics and the law

If self-regulation is problematic, does it then make sense to go outside this model and to involve the law of the land in the ethical behaviour or transgressions of the professional? Currently, there is no legislation within the United Kingdom to enforce registration of therapists or to provide redress for dissatisfied clients. A private members bill on the subject failed to be passed. Anyone at present then can set up as a therapist.

Some moves are afoot to challenge this, and the UK Standing Conference on Psychotherapy is campaigning for a registration procedure, and for sexual exploitation to be formally recognised as malpractice and as a criminal offence.

My own view is somewhat less didactic, which emanates from my view of the problem as fairly complex and from a degree of cynicism based on knowledge of how the legal system works with abuse in other areas. One woman who did try to take action was advised not to by two solicitors because there were no witnesses. On the other hand, I can see a case for making such abuse a transgression of society's morals and the legal system at least adds weight to this perspective.

We might note that under the 1983 Mental Health Act, sex between female patients and male staff is illegal and carries serious penalties. This refers specifically to sexual intercourse, and it is significant that female staff and male patients do not have the same protection under the act. Despite these limitations, it does offer precedence for a legal acknowledgement that vulnerable people may need protection from professionals.

Given that we do not at present have this behaviour outlawed on a wider scale, it may again be useful to look briefly at the American experience. Several American states have now legislated along the lines of sexual intimacy in the therapeutic relationship being established as rape. It needs only for it to be established that sexual intimacy has occurred, not that it was necessarily damaging, for action to be taken against the therapist.[2] This in itself can be problematic, however, and is by no means cut and dried.

Austin et al. (1990) give some examples of successful legal action for malpractice. It seems that to be successful, sexual intimacy must be proved, and that the statute should specifically include sexual intimacy as an instance of unprofessional conduct, thus allowing a charge of malpractice to be made. One plaintiff successfully sued a psychiatrist for having a sexual relationship with his (the plaintiff's) wife during the course of his treatment (Austin et al., 1990: 149). This situation was seen as a betrayal of trust with the implication that it would be detrimental for the client's current or future therapy. In the American courts, it seems that consent is not accepted by the courts on the grounds that it is likely to be influenced by transference, and that the plea that sex is a part of therapy or began after the therapy has ended is unlikely to form a successful defence.

This subject is worthy of fuller discussion and will undoubtedly receive attention from the relevant professions. It is worth noting that as far as we know, this course of action has not been successful in reducing the incidence of exploitative practice, though it perhaps serves the purpose of validating the client's experience.

Areas not covered

Finally, we have the areas which are not fully covered in professional codes of ethics. Two major areas spring to mind. The first is where a professional knows of other professionals who are, or suspected to be, behaving in an exploitative manner. This seems largely uncovered in the ethical codes, although it seems that many workers would welcome some guidelines here. There are exceptions, one being the British Psychological Society, who state that members should:

> where they suspect misconduct by a professional colleague which cannot be resolved or remedied after discussion with the colleague concerned,

take steps to bring that misconduct to the attention of those charged with the responsibility to investigate it, doing so without malice and with no breaches of confidentiality other than those necessary to the proper investigatory processes. (1985: 5.7)

This is also a requirement made of nurses by the United Kingdom Central Council, the governing body. The procedure here is to report suspicions to the Standards and Ethics Committee.

Within the British Association for Counselling, there is a clause in the code of practice which states that:

If a counsellor suspects misconducts by another counsellor which cannot be resolved or remedied after discussion with the counsellor concerned, they should implement the Complaints Procedure, doing so without breaches of confidentiality other than those necessary for investigating the complaint. (1990: 2.4.2)

What is not clear is what support is available where there is conflict between client confidentiality and the responsibility to report.

Two people responded to my research from this perspective, that is, 'being in the know'. One was a social worker who worked alongside a psychiatrist specialising in work with adolescents. She and other staff were disturbed by some of the comments that adolescent girls made about how he touched them. Some were singled out for gifts of jewellery on special occasions. Various moves had been made to air the misgivings, but no action could be taken as none of the girls actually made a complaint. This psychiatrist, a man in his fifties, eventually divorced his wife and married a patient in her teens.

The social worker in question felt helpless, as the chair of the Area Health Authority (AHA) in question had been approached with no results. The difficulty was very much in having nothing tangible to work with. She and co-workers attempted to get general practitioners to refer elsewhere, although this was difficult. She stated that the situation 'filled everybody with guilt', and left them feeling that there was nowhere to go. There was also the dilemma caused by recognising that he seemed to be very successful in treating some of his clients. Frustration was the major feeling expressed here.

Another woman I interviewed, herself an experienced counsellor, found herself in the unenviable position of counselling a client, himself a therapist, who disclosed inappropriate sexual behaviour with clients. She had known this man professionally and had had some therapy with him some time previously. On his first request for her to see him, she expressed doubt about this being appropriate because of the possibility of blurred boundaries. He then requested that she see him for an assessment interview, then to refer on, and, with reservations, she agreed.

The main content of this interview was his 'confession' that over a period of some years, he had been having sexual relationships with clients in the consulting room during therapy sessions. This was revealed after a contract of confidentiality had been agreed. He expressed fear of being reported, and 'to some extent I think he was also worried about the compulsiveness of his behaviour'. This posed a great dilemma for the counsellor concerned. Her general anxiety was exacerbated by having referred clients to him, one of whom at least had been previously sexually abused. She also knew that he worked with incest survivors, who she felt to be a particularly vulnerable group, with their feelings of love becoming eroticised, so that 'the therapist needs to be scrupulous'.

This counsellor felt very strongly that therapists who abuse should be reported to the appropriate governing body, but in this situation she felt unable to do so. I am struck by two points here, one is perhaps the strength of feeling that he at least was able to trust her with the information. This is perhaps a point of faith that recognition is essential to change, even if that change is not imminent. The second point, and perhaps the major one here, is her own lack of support at this time, which perhaps reflects on the agency. It seems to me that all counsellors should have access to supervision, which must be recognised by the employer. Again I would refer to contracting. My own limits of confidentiality include the understanding that at my discretion I will share case material with a supervisor. At the very least, this allows for some resolution of dilemmas over ethical issues.

This is a major area of concern. American researchers conclude that many professionals know of (suspected) misconduct by others, and that they at best feel helpless in the situation and at worst are collusive with it.

This leads to a final unconsidered area, where therapists know of exploitative practice revealed by their client. This may present a dilemma of confidentiality and protection of a wider group. Some participants in my research are in the process of working through their feelings, goals and possible courses of action with new therapists. At least two of those I know are considering filing complaints.

In the United States, there is suggestion of mandatory exposure by the therapist in this situation. The difficulty here is that this may be disempowering to the client and seen as a further betrayal of trust. There are no easy solutions here, but it does seem essential to consider the problem.

Conclusions

We can see from this chapter that there are many grey areas as to what may constitute ethical norms, but that we do however try to operate some ethical norms, and that the consequences of breaking them may affect more than just the individuals concerned. Different situations – for example, counselling, supervision, training – require different parameters. Ethical committees exist to protect the client, yet are themselves fraught with difficulties. At present there is no legal solution offered in Britain.

In my view it is unlikely that we can ever make totally clear and consistent judgement. I am reminded of more than one relationship which started out with a counselling dimension and has ended in something of other dimensions between two equal adults. I would hesitate to make any sort of judgement which prohibits who may, for example, fall in love with whom, and which totally prohibits any kind of sexual relationship at some time after the counselling relationship has ended.

It is also clear that clients must be protected from unethical and exploitative practice by the counsellor. It seems that consistent and full guidelines must be provided so that if a practitioner subscribes to a particular code, they must be seen to be held to the conditions of that code. At the very least, this offers clients a frame of reference, and at best, a safeguard for themselves.

It seems that useful clarification could be made on several points within professional codes of ethics. For example:

- A more detailed synopsis of what might constitute sexual behaviour.
- An ethical requirement to report colleagues who are thought to be exploiting, with a middle forum between the options of addressing the colleague and making a complaint.
- A recommendation on a minimum period of time between the termination of a counselling relationship and the initiation of a sexual relationship.
- A recommendation on a minimum period of time between the termination of a training or supervisory relationship and the initiation of a sexual relationship.

The British Association for Counselling has amended its *Code of Ethics and Practice for Counsellors* (1990) to read in consideration of this point. Item 2.2.6 now reads:

> Counsellors must not exploit clients financially, sexually, emotionally or in any other way. Engaging in sexual activity with current clients within

12 weeks of the end of the counselling relationship is unethical. If the counselling relationship has been over an extended period of time or been working in-depth a much longer 'cooling off' period is required and a lifetime prohibition on a future sexual relationship with the client may be more appropriate.

The wording reflects the complexity of what might constitute a counselling relationship. For example, is there a difference between a single encounter and a long-term contract? Nevertheless, the inclusion recognises that there is a principle to be addressed and will no doubt engender more dialogue on the subject.

There is no doubt that the more clarity within the professions, the better, particularly when it is in a form which is accessible to clients. This leads to the final point worth making – that counsellors and therapists be required ethically to tell clients that they will not be entering into a social or sexual relationship with them. Food for thought, perhaps.

Note

1 No recommended period of time will be seen as universally acceptable. I also recognise the limits of codes of ethics as a prohibitor. However, in addressing the principle, six months is suggested in recognition of the loss involved in the termination of a therapeutic relationship. Although there is no determined time span for any individual's grieving process, it is normally accepted that the acute stage of grief occurs within the first six months. If we appropriate the grief model to the termination of the therapeutic relationship, then we might reasonably predict that after a six month period the (ex)client will be better placed to rationally consider whether they wish to initiate contact on a social basis with the former counsellor. Such initiation must be the prerogative of the ex-client only, not the counsellor.

2 For sources and further discussion, see Bouhoutsos (1985), and Holroyd and Bouhoutsos (1985) and Leesfield (1987).

8

IMPLICATIONS IN PRACTICE

It would seem to be useful to offer some suggestions for implications for practice in three areas. The first is in looking at the counselling process itself, and to examine some examples of how and where the potential for exploitation enters the arena. Secondly, it will be helpful to look at how supervision may benefit the practitioner and hence the client. Models of practice for both these areas are presented visually as well as illustrated, and are offered as possibilities rather than prescriptions. Each is underpinned by a belief that any complex process is made easier and hence more accessible to both practitioner and client if it is broken down into a framework or structure. This minimises the opportunity for mysticism, where the parties involved do not understand the process, and for either intentional or unintentional exploitation. Both models have been co-developed with my colleague Graham Dexter. The language in this chapter is deliberately generic. I use the terms counsellor, therapist and worker to make the point that these models of working may apply to many of the helping professions.

Finally, some comments on the training process and some specific exercises are offered as exemplars of how we might start to address the relevant issues. This is by no means an attempt to give a full and comprehensive guide, rather to stimulate discussion, fuel ideas and raise awareness of the issues to be reviewed.

A model for working with sexuality and sexual abuse in counselling and therapy

In working with sexually abused clients, experience has demonstrated that many of the issues which arise for the client are not unique to this particular client group, although there may be sharp focus on particular concerns. However, in training and supervising mental health workers, it seems that the issues for them may be specific and feel either unique or threatening. The following model (see Model 8.1), then, acknowledges this perception.

Although originally developed as a paradigm for working with

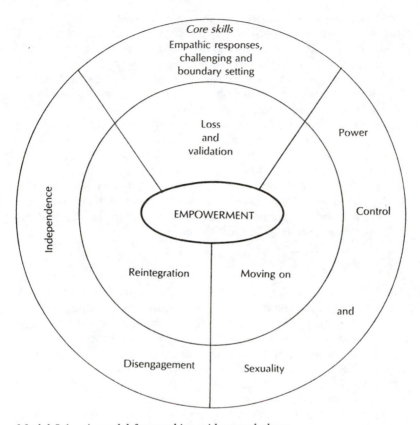

Model 8.1   *A model for working with sexual abuse*

© Dexter and Russell, 1991

sexual abuse, the model seems relevant to the focus of this book for two reasons. The first is that many informants to available research indicate that they had encountered previous sexual abuse, whether or not this was the primary focus of the counselling at the time. Secondly, the issues of sexuality and power which are highlighted within the model are pertinent to the exploitative practitioner and to the potential victim.

Like many counselling and therapeutic models, this one is loosely structured as tripartite. The centre of the model is empowerment. This acknowledges that for clients who have been sexually abused and/or are vulnerable to exploitation, the ability to take their own power and to control their own destiny is of paramount importance. If this is recognised from the outset, then the risk of exploitation is reduced. This is true for any client, but has a particular poignancy for those who have been abused as they will have had one or more forceful experiences of being overwhelmed and out of control. Regaining self-control is central to the therapeutic process, and recognition of this on the part of the worker is helpful.

The concept of empowerment is also important for the worker. Whenever the worker is thrown by what is happening within the counselling process, he or she is vulnerable to feeling either deskilled, confused or threatened. In this situation, the worker may become disempowered and take one of two courses of action. One is to fail to address the relevant issues appropriately, hence the client receives an inadequate service which may itself feel exploitative. This was demonstrated by those participants who felt that sexual issues were 'opened up' and then ignored. Alternatively, the worker may be tempted to wield all the power in the relationship and thus disempower or exploit the client.

Stage one

The initial *concerns* for the worker are to exercise the basic skills of empathic listening, the conditions of genuineness and unconditional positive regard, and the skills of effective challenging. The first *task* of the worker is to acknowledge the responsibilities for clear boundary setting and to put this understanding into action by negotiating a clear contract of working. Again, while this is important for all clients it has a particular puissance where a client has been previously sexually abused and had his or her boundaries invaded. The client may then have an established pattern of making unclear personal boundaries, as we have seen in some of the accounts within this work. It is, then, all the more important for the worker to assume responsiblity for clarity and consistency here.

Many clients may be unfamiliar with counselling and thus it is up to the practitioner to set the context and scene and to outline limitations of time, frequency of sessions, ability of the counsellor, responsibilities of each party, confidentiality and personal relationship. This may require something like the following considerations.

Frequency and length of sessions needs to be established clearly, so that there is a reminder that this is a working relationship. Once established, the contract needs to be maintained in the knowledge that once sessions are allowed to occur outside these boundaries, the client may begin to feel that they are in some way unique or special. Since counsellors do have time limits on their work, it is worth them asking themselves what is special about this client if they fail to observe the contract.

From the outset, the notion of dependency needs to be recognised. My own preference is to contract an initial number of sessions at the end of which the process may be reviewed. This may reassure the client that there is no obligation to return if he or she does not feel we are working well together. Conversely, if the practitioner is struggling to work effectively, it offers the opportunity for the practitioner to identify this. It also offers the opportunity to measure what seems to be helpful and help the client to identify what is changing and how. Moreover, it again reminds both worker and client that this is a working alliance towards a purposeful goal.

If a client seems particularly vulnerable, the worker may feel tempted to offer open emergency access. This may take the form of offering a personal phone number for any time, a strategy which many practitioners seem to adopt at some point. Again, such a strategy indicates some degree of high personal involvement, and while understanding the feelings of concern which may be present in some working relationships, such lack of boundaries immediately introduces a 'specialness'. This is not to say that in some situations it might be helpful to develop emergency strategies using services available – it is the personal indispensability which is at question.

It is also useful for the counsellor to outline to the client the counsellor's view of the process and his or her responsibility within it. In some ways, this is quite difficult if the client has no knowledge of the subject, but even so it is worth stating. So that, for example, it would be relevant for me to state that I am a counsellor and not a psychotherapist, that I see my task as to facilitate the client in exploring and understanding personal issues and to develop ways of managing his or her life in a more fulfilling way. I might also state that I do not have the ability or desire to solve the client's problems, but that I see our relationship as a working alliance in which I will use my skills and experience as fully as possible to assist the client with problem-solving. For the client's part, it is his or her responsibility to raise issues considered relevant, to turn up at appropriate times, and to do homework between times. This may seem simplistic, but gives a flavour of the attempt to demystify from the outset. As time goes on, this can be referred back to where necessary, and fuller insight be gained.

The final boundaries which need to be set are the ethical boundaries, specifically of confidentiality and of personal relationship. This is seen as essential for both worker and client. It is highly beneficial for both parties if the counsellor states at the outset that this is a specific and purposeful activity and that there will be no relationship of friendship or sexual contact. This may feel strange for the client if there were no expectations in this direction, but it is my experience that any query which this elicits is far outweighed by the safety created by the clarity. One male colleague who also uses this approach has twice been told by female clients that this contract has allowed them to freely discuss sexual issues at a later stage in the process.

Such clarity also aids the worker. Sexual attraction may be felt at an initial meeting, and the clear verbalising of boundaries is a public statement that such attraction will not be acted upon. If he or she feels such attraction, the statement may also remind the worker that this may be an issue and enable such recognition to be taken to supervision if necessary.

On confidentiality, again the counsellor needs to communicate the limits of the concept. This might go something like:

> It seems important for me to tell you that whatever we talk about and work with here will remain confidential. There are two exceptions to this: one is that I have a supervisor and may need to discuss our work with her. If this happens, I would not use your name but might need to discuss some of the issues. This would be to help me give you the best service. I also follow a code of ethics and if at any time I was concerned that you were a danger to yourself or to anyone else, I would not tie myself to being bound by confidentiality. Should this happen, I would discuss my concern with you.

The client may want clarification on any of this, and may need to come back to it at any point within the process. It is important though that no false illusions are created, so that a position of respect may be established from the start. To betray confidence when the client has no knowledge that this might happen can be devastating, as it replicates previous experiences of betrayal of trust. This is particularly relevant in disclosures of sexual abuse.

These then are some of the major components of a sample contract. It is not exhaustive, and is intended as being illustrative.

Once this is negotiated, important issues for the client at this stage are that personal feelings should be validated through the active skills of the worker. Careful listening here enables the worker to pick up any cues which may indicate potential attraction or particular sexual patterns. A high degree of awareness may help indicate where the likelihood of transference or potential repetition of patterns may occur. This is also true of the counsellor's self-awareness – 'am I aware of any attraction?', 'does this person remind me of significant events or people in my own life?', etc. This point will be referred to later in the section on supervision.

I said earlier that challenging is one of the essential skills of this work, and I use it in four respects particularly which have specific focus within this work. The first respect is that of challenging the client's strengths, enabling the client to see that he or she has

resources and ways of dealing with things which have been used
before and which can be called upon again. For example, consider
the following situation. A client may be bemoaning the ending of a
time when his or her sexual desires were completely fulfilled, and be
feeling devoid of satisfaction at the present. The client's perspective
of the problem may be that there is no suitable partner to provide
fulfilment, and thus feels depressed and isolated. There may well be
a reality in the preferred scenario including a partner on the scene.
However, it is also useful for the counsellor to challenge with the
perspective that the client has previously been able to tap into his or
her sexual qualities, it was not just the power of previous situations.
For example:

> So you know that you are able to experience and express your desires
> when you feel the trust to be able to do so, and you know that you are
> capable of arousal and satisfaction. You would like to be able to be in
> touch with this ability of yours again.

This makes for approaching the problem as one being under the
client's control, and to reduce feelings of helplessness. Moreover, in
relation to exploitative practice, it is useful to keep this focus rather
than focus on the power of another to awaken the said feelings. This
is the sort of situation which may become exploitative if there is
attraction between client and counsellor, and perhaps particularly if
the counsellor identifies with the sexual frustration.

Such a response may sound glib without the conditions of
genuineness and respect which must be in place in order to work
effectively. Gerard Egan (1990) states that the helper needs to earn
the right to challenge through demonstrating such qualities and
conditions, and this seems the best way to put it. On the other hand,
earning the right to challenge if a practitioner is both open and
skilled does not have to be a lengthy process, and challenging
strengths will be enabling to the client from the beginning.

A second form of challenge which is particularly pertinent to
issues of sexuality and power is in using the skill of immediacy.
Immediacy, well documented elsewhere (see for example Egan,
1990), enables the counsellor to check out any feelings, emotions or
thoughts which he or she is conscious of but wants to explore. For
example, in the case of sexual feelings, there might be hints that the
client is attracted to the counsellor, or feelings of sexual arousal on
the counsellor's side. This may need to be acknowledged and
clarified as to their source.

My own experience might illustrate the point. Having worked
with a heterosexual male client for four sessions, the material under

discussion had become focused on his sexual feelings and his relationships with women. In the fourth session the dialogue was something like:

> *Client*: I always find myself heavily attracted to women who are intelligent and seem to be strong, and I am frequently attracted to women who are counsellors.
> *Counsellor*: I notice that you look embarrassed when you say that, Paul, and sense some tension between us.
> *Client*: Well yes, I do feel a bit tense.
> *Counsellor*: I'm wondering whether that has to do with how you feel towards me.
> *Client*: Well yes, I feel awkward because I feel attracted to you.

Having acknowledged the attraction, we were able to work with it constructively rather than have an area which we could not speak about. The immediacy was in my recognising the tension, and coupled with some degree of empathy meant that the client was relieved rather than threatened by the intervention. I was able to accept his feelings and he felt secure within the bounds of our contract.

A third form of challenge is in challenging faulty thinking. Going on the lines of Ellis' rational-emotive therapy, there needs to be a belief that people's emotions are influenced by the internal messages, or self-talk, which they give to themselves (Ellis and Whiteley, 1979). This can be particularly powerful where a client has been sexually abused, and where they feel guilty. Thought patterns may go along the lines of:

> I aroused him (her) sexually and that is why they abused me. It must have been something I said or did, therefore it is my fault.

We saw this repeated in clients' accounts of both previous abuse and exploitation within counselling and therapy. Moreover, it was colluded with by practitioners in telling clients that they were very seductive.

An alertness to faulty thinking patterns can help the worker be immediately in touch with appropriate challenge, for example:

> You are attractive and X might have felt aroused by you. Nevertheless, the responsibility for the subsequent actions was his (hers) and you had the right to say no. He (she) exercised some choice in dealing with his (her) feelings. It seems you feel in some way to blame, as if you were responsible for his (her) choices and actions, yet this doesn't seem logical.

Depending on the specific issue and the relationship in place, it may be appropriate for the counsellor to state, if finding someone attractive, that there is no intention of acting on that attraction. This can itself challenge the faulty thinking, demonstrating that someone's attractiveness, or even attempts at seduction, are not irresistible and that the other party can exercise intentionality and control.

A fourth form of challenge hinges on the recognition that as individuals we function within a variety of social and societal systems which influence our thinking. Challenge here is informed by our ability to know and to contest various myths. In some ways these parallel the faulty thinking pattern, but it is helpful to challenge in the wider, or the more abstract, myths such as the male sexual imperative. By this I mean the notion that man with erection must be satisfied, therefore women ask for it. There are several such myths and some will be found in the section on training. It is helpful for workers to be consciously familiar with these and to be able to challenge when they are expressed or seen as influencing the client's thinking.

Through operating the skills of empathic response coupled with these challenging skills, the counsellor is able to validate the client's feelings and to begin to challenge self-defeating patterns of thought or behaviour, thus helping the client to accept his or her feelings as appropriate. When working with known previous sexual abuse, it is helpful to facilitate the client's feelings of grief which are concomitant with the hidden losses commonly recognised as being associated with such an experience.[1]

While it is not appropriate to go into detail here, it is worth noting that it is useful for counsellors to acquaint themselves with current literature on sexual abuse generally to help themselves to be alert to symptoms or manifestations which may (and this must be approached with caution) suggest that previous abuse has taken place. Thus the counsellor is alert to any possibility of acting out old patterns within the working relationship. Several participants in my research realised after the exploitative experience had taken place that they had in fact been previously abused, and were angry that the worker had failed to spot the signs of this being the case.

Stage two

The second stage of Model 8.1 is still fuelled by the same skills, but with a deeper working relationship in place the focus of the issues for worker and client will shift. Having identified and explored past and current issues, the focus for the client will be on goal-setting and moving on. This will entail careful recognition that the very act of goal-setting may identify more work on the past and present, but that the setting of the goals, and the agenda to be followed, is part of the client's recovery. This part of the process is particularly tied up with client empowerment, in recognising that whatever problems or difficulties have existed, there is the possibility for change, and that, moreover, this is under the client's control.

The skills required for this part of the model build on those already operated, and need to be matched by the counsellor's ability to trust the client and to resist the temptation to wield power. The counsellor must be able to recognise that the past and present need not control the client's future, that the client can change.

At this stage there is the opportunity to resist any sexual acting out which may occur, if for example the client suggests sexual contact with the counsellor as part of his or her desired goal. The counsellor then has the opportunity to challenge the client by resisting any approach with warmth and in safety. This then gives the client the opportunity of a new experience where acceptance does not have to involve sexual behaviour. For some clients, this new possibility helps them to generate alternative behaviour patterns which will be more fulfilling in the long term than previous patterns have been.

The middle stage seems to be the biggest area of confrontation for some workers. As the research has shown, the relationship is by now more intimate, and the client may be exploring sexual behaviour, attitudes and feelings in order to identify strengths and to picture a preferred scenario. This itself may entail the identification of how the client might like to feel sexually, and at this point the potential for exploitation is again highlighted. Thus the need for the counsellor to exercise self-awareness and caution regarding his or her own responses and attitudes.

If the counsellor is aware of leading the content, or feeling sexually aroused, then these issues must be faced and taken to supervision. One way to combat this is to stay with accurate empathic response to the client's narrative and resist the urge to be curious. For example, the client's exploration of a preferred scenario may tap into areas where the counsellor is also unfulfilled. Or the client may wish for close physical contact, in order to feel loved and valued. If the counsellor discovers the urge to offer close hugs, or to have the client on the knees, or sitting at the feet (all of which are present in the research), then I would suggest that the counsellor is exercising the unwise use of power, perhaps for personal sexual gratification, and that the ultimate outcome of such behaviour is contrary to the client's interests. No doubt this is a contestable point of view and is presented simplistically in this context, but evidence so far suggests that caution is wise.

Stage three

Having identified where to move on to next, the task for the client is now that of reintegration. Having moved through a transitional phase and identified what he or she wants, various strategies may need to be explored to bring this to fruition. Commonly this may include dealing with unfinished business, expressing hitherto hidden emotions, and some behavioural programmes. Such activities help the client to integrate past experiences into the present and to accept conflicting and ambivalent emotions.

The issue for the worker is now to disengage from the client's life with an acceptance of any emotions which this may provoke for either party. This is an opportunity for the client to face an ending, a goodbye, in a whole sense, to express positive and negative emotions. The counsellor must be able to accept any anger or sadness about this without becoming entangled in the process, or misidentifying the emotions for something other than the counselling relationship. Here, being able to refer to the clear contract made at the beginning can aid the process for both parties.

The counsellor may also feel the loss of the client if they have worked closely together. It is important to be able to accept and express this within the appropriate context and perspective, and here one of the dangers is the counsellor's inability to let the client go. Should this happen, then again the counsellor needs to check what it is that the client is providing for the counsellor which is inappropriate. This is again an opportunity for reflection on any issue of power or sexuality which is unresolved. Supervision is again of paramount importance at this stage.

Comments

The model described above is one approach only, and it must be stressed that it is an exemplar rather than a 'how-to-do-it' model, which would be the subject of another work. The reality is that issues of sexuality and power may enter the therapeutic relationship at any stage. The strength of this model, however, lies in the recognition that the counsellor's own issues of sexuality and power lie at the heart of exploitative practice, and that a consistent self-awareness and monitoring are helpful as preventive measures. The whole process is complex, and the model can only work with skilled use and with a thorough understanding of the therapeutic process in greater detail. Nevertheless, it may be useful in aiding consideration of the issues under review and in stimulating counsellors to find strategies which fit their way of working. It may also be useful to people in the client seat if they know what should *not* be happening in the therapeutic relationship.

A client-centred model of supervision

However sensitive and aware the practitioner is to any specific issues within the counselling process, he or she will inevitably have blind spots. I have repeatedly suggested that effective supervision is a keystone to good practice, and this is where blind spots may be brought to awareness, and where support may be found towards making the most effective and ethically correct way of working.

The model of supervision which I co-developed and use is informed by my own experience of supervision – as supervisee, supervisor and trainer in a variety of statutory and voluntary agencies. Looking back, it is easy to see what felt safe to discuss, what felt dangerous, and how enabling or not the process was to open disclosure.

It seems helpful to see supervision, like counselling, as a clear and purposeful activity for which supervisors and supervisees may need to be trained in order to maximise its potential – it is more than either accountability or 'talking through'. The model is not intended as a device for structuring supervisors or supervisees into a straitjacket, or for reducing the flexibility or imagination of skilled workers – on the contrary, it may enhance the latter qualities.

Within this context, I shall use the model to illustrate how a genuine and respectful supervisory relationship, fuelled by a high level of communication skills, may provide a forum for debrief and exploration of issues of sexuality and power, thus ensuring the ultimate goal of benefiting the client. Some understanding of supervision must be assumed here, and the model in its full form may be found elsewhere (see Dexter and Russell, 1991).

The model (see Model 8.2) consists of a six-stage circular process, dependent on skilled facilitation. The relevant elements are:

1   Mutual contracting.
2   Casework analysis:
    (a)   identifying current problems, issues, concerns and situations;
    (b)   identifying current strengths, qualities, talents and skills;
    (c)   identifying current intra- and interpersonal issues.
3   Goal-setting.

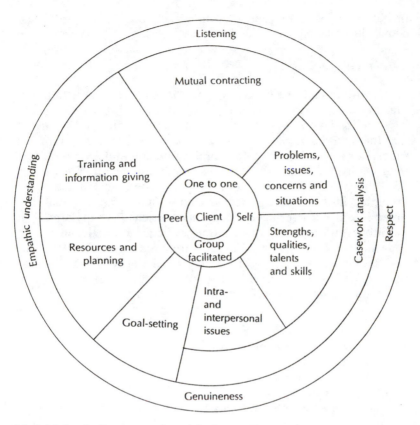

Model 8.2   *A client-centred model of supervision*
© Dexter and Russell, 1991

4   Resources and planning.
5   Training and information giving.
6   Mutual contracting.

Skills and values acknowledged in the outer perimeter of Model 8.2 operate from a counselling philosophy, which underpins a belief that effective supervision is a facilitative process, hopefully enriching to all participants, rather than a mechanical procedure. The major functions of the supervisor are seen as twofold. One is to structure according to the mutual goals of supervision, which may need to incorporate agency expectations. The second, and equal in importance, is to recognise the need for supervisees to talk through any emotions, difficulties and anxieties. The process has been linked directly to the counselling process (Tschudin, 1987). While this process is seen as relevant, it is important to refrain from simply counselling the supervisee and hence confusing boundaries.

Mutual contracting

Within the model, the welfare of the client is seen as central, and thus as the supervisor's main responsibility. Supervisors, therefore, have an obligation to get the best deal for the client, and to ensure that the supervisee is operating 'good practice', to the best of the supervisor's knowledge. Implicit in this fundamental premise is that there is also the responsibility to the supervisee to provide systematic supervision of a high quality, and where appropriate, for example, in line management supervision, to ensure that the supervisee is not overloaded or agency-abused. Perhaps central to this process is the notion of a contract, which is mutually negotiated and which clarifies standards, expectations and what to do if it is felt that the client is not getting a fair deal. This is why mutual contracting is seen as the first stage of the supervision process.

A typical contract may focus on the following:

- Particular skills or approaches.
- Individual goals of supervision.
- Agency goals and expectations.
- Personal/professional/practice debrief.
- Timing for supervision.
- Extent of confidentiality.
- The supervisor's responsibility to monitor the ethical context of the supervisee's practice.
- Boundaries of the relationship.
- Length of contract.

While it is not appropriate to elucidate this fully within this work, it may be helpful to look at confidentiality and ethical issues in slightly more depth.

The complete confidential contract may not always be possible or desirable. Bohart and Todd cite the California Supreme Court Tarasoff decision (1971), as a useful example of the need to have exceptions to complete confidentiality. In this case of a client who was intending to and eventually did kill their daughter, it was ruled that 'private privilege ends where public peril begins' (1988: 345). This principle may be related to supervision. As a general guideline, the supervisee's client is also the supervisor's vicarious responsibility, and must remain the priority. Client endangerment may be substituted for public peril in this context.

Client endangerment in this framework may relate to the sexual exploitation of the client by the worker. The worker must know from the beginning of the supervisory relationship where he or she stands if there is a sexual encounter with a client. This will tie into understanding the ethical codes of conduct by which the supervisor is bound. Thus if the supervisee knows from the outset that sexual liaison will not be colluded with, then the supervisee understands where confidentiality may be breached.

How this might happen also needs some careful negotiation. The supervisor's responsibility is to ensure that as far as possible, the supervisee is enabled rather than disabled. If the supervisee feels that he or she is in danger of transgressing boundaries and knows that disclosure of this will result in being immmediately reported to a disciplinary body, then no disclosure will take place. Thus this will be counterproductive for the client.

Therefore the responsibility within the contract is that in the eventuality of the supervisor judging behaviour as unethical, then this would be discussed with the supervisee, and reporting would be one option. There is then a matter for negotiated clinical judgement which might hinge on questions such as:

- Does the supervisee know that his or her practice is unethical?
- Does any increase in knowledge change the behaviour?
- How far has it gone?
- Is the supervisee wanting to initiate a sexual relationship or is he or she at the pre-relationship stage where there is still a desire to prevent it?
- Is the supervisee taking time out of work?
- What is the supervisee's motivation in making the disclosure?
- Are there things for the supervisee to work out constructively with the client so that the client does not feel suddenly abandoned?

There are no clear cut answers, but the ethical code subscribed to is acknowledged and the responsibility is to follow it in the best way possible in the interests of the client. The supervisee must know this from the outset. Behaviour which intentionally transgresses will not be colluded with, and this links to the section on training and information giving.

While this may sound too unclear for some palates, the framework within which it operates is one where a climate of trust is being established. If this is really so, then disclosure will be made at the pre-exploitative stage. If supervisors are straitjacketed on the other hand, then the client may be more at risk, and the supervisee may be treated disrespectfully.

This echoes the experience of the participant in this research who disclosed to her supervisor that she and a client had terminated their working contract because of sexual attraction. They had agreed that the client may contact her some weeks later with a view to a social relationship. The disclosure cost this counsellor an immediate report to an ethical committee. Whatever the rights and wrongs, her summary opinion was that she wished she had not made the disclosure. Another example is of a worker within a statutory agency who disclosed that he was aroused by some work on child sexual abuse. Immediate suspension and subsequent dismissal followed. Being satisfied that the motivation behind the disclosure was to seek help and secure safety for the clients, I wonder how many other workers are secretly aroused and find no place to disclose, a practice far more dangerous in my view.

Other ethical considerations which may need to be considered might involve the relationship between supervisor and supervisee. This is an opportunity to model appropriate boundaries, and to stipulate that the relationship will not be one of sexual dimensions. Friendship is more difficult to be definitive about, as there is no reason why skilled practitioners are not able to operate their skills within a specific negotiated framework with people that they know. Nevertheless, it is encumbent on the supervisor to set clear boundaries about what is discussed where, and to keep the supervisory relationship separate from any other professional or social relationship.

The supervisee has the responsibility for using supervision effectively. This will mean developing the courage and ability for disclosure of issues and concerns, the skills of case management and prioritisation, and the ability to analyse positive interventions. Although the right to withhold disclosures remain the supervisee's, long-term inability to disclose or confront issues may, at its most extreme, result in forfeiture of the right to practice. This is perhaps something for the supervisor to be alert to – what is the supervisee not saying, and how might the supervisor be more enabling?

Casework analysis

(a) Identifying current problems, issues, concerns and situations. Current issues may be particular cases where the supervisee just feels stuck, where he or she needs to review intervention for assessment purposes, or specific problems or concerns such as client dependence, overload, time management, administrative concerns, or the appropriateness of any particular techniques or interventions. Within this space, the supervisee may identify situations where it is felt that no progress is being made with a client despite much work.

Exploration may engender the identification of different techniques which may be necessary. The importance for current purposes is that it may also provoke recognition that there is a collusion from the practitioner's point of view which may illustrate an inappropriate use of (or failure to use) personal power. For example, it may be that the counsellor is very comfortable and enjoys the client so much that he or she does not want to let the client go, or has some vested interest in retaining the relationship.

(b) Identifying current strengths, qualities, talents and skills.   If the supervisor has listened carefully to the supervisee's current issues, it should be possible to identify the skills, qualities and strengths that the supervisee has available. The supervisor should be able gently to challenge clearer insights into what is potentially available within the resources of worker, agency and client, in order to move on within the process. Often supervisees need reminding at this point of the objectives of the contract with the client. This is another opportunity to identify inappropriate use of power or control. It is also a chance to challenge supervisees to see themselves undiluted, with their deficiencies, weaknesses and mistakes set alongside their strengths, talents, skills, personal qualities and resources. This implies a recognition of them as developing workers, and may help to counter the feelings of helplessness or disempowerment which have been suggested as being unconstructive, or even potentially exploitative.

(c) Identifying intra- and interpersonal issues.   Within every case discussed will be elements of the interpersonal dynamic between worker and client, that may require debrief. This can be as low key as 'I wonder why I like this client more than this one', to more high profile feelings such as 'I hate seeing X, he (she) really winds me up', or 'I feel sexually attracted to this client'. In other words, the interpersonal issues that require debriefing are the thoughts, feelings and behaviours that are stimulated between the two parties. It may be that there are some barriers, anxieties or difficulties that require identifying and working through before the relationship can progress. In some instances, particularly where the worker may be involved against the wishes of the client, it may be that hostility may always be encountered for which the worker needs support. Equally important may be the intrapersonal issues for the worker, such as 'What thoughts, feelings and behaviours are evoked for me through working with this client?', 'How do I feel when I contemplate this interview?' and 'How do I feel when I come out?'

If this space for the examination of personal issues is highlighted, and if it is overtly recognised by the supervisor that they exist, then the supervisee may find it easier to examine his or her own practice from this perspective.

In terms of sexual practice, this will be the opportunity to disclose any interpersonal feelings of attraction to the client, or of feeling that the client is attracted to the worker. A typical disclosure might be:

> I noticed that when she began to discuss sexual material I diverted the subject elsewhere. I felt quite uncomfortable. Now that I begin to talk about it, I realise that I am anxious in case I become aroused. I'm worried then that she will think I'm attracted to her – I'm not sure if I am or not.

Such disclosure will facilitate exploration of the issues and enable strategies to be put in place which will encourage safety for client and worker. Without it, there is the possibility of voyeurism or exploitation.

Similarly, the possibility of intrapersonal issues arising is highlighted here. So for example a counsellor might notice that:

> As she began to talk about her abuse, I realised that I was becoming both fascinated and panicky. I felt almost scared of what was coming next. Thinking about this in the week made me think that perhaps I was overidentifying, and maybe I need some more support about my own experiences of abuse.

Failure to exercise such awareness may result in the counsellor depersonalising or distancing from the client's experience, which may be experienced as abusive.

The above examples give the impression that we are all extremely self-aware and miss nothing, but of course in reality it will be the working relationship within supervision that facilitates disclosure. Moreover, some interpersonal dynamic may be present which is not immediately identified as sexual. In my own supervision, I examined a relationship with a client which I knew was uncomfortable, but no more. It was the process of supervision which helped me to realise that I had assumed a defensive posture as the client involved challenged my boundaries, including that of sexuality. I might or might not have got to this on my own, but the 'third ear' of my supervisor helped to clarify it for me.

Issues within this section may not be related directly to the specific relationship with a particular client, but rooted in doubts about personal competence. Most counsellors, therapists and helpers experience the personal need to be helpful, the often overwhelming need to demonstrate skills, success or progress, or the frustrations of their limitations. The opportunity to air such feelings helps to retain a realistic view of what may be achieved and therefore help the worker to offer the client his or her best.

Goal-setting

This stage of supervision is crucial although it is often under-used in systematic supervision. There appear to be some vital questions that need addressing at this stage that make a significant contribution to effective supervision:

- What are you trying to achieve with this client?

On occasion, where workers are involved with whole families, they may need to remind themselves of who the client is:

- What do you believe the client is trying to achieve?
- What are your preferred outcomes?
- Are any of the above unethical, or contrary to either your own or the client's welfare?
- Are your goals compatible with those of the organisation you work for?
- If you continue with what you are doing, will the interests of the client, yourself and the organisation be best served?
- If the answer to any of the above creates dissonance, how might this be resolved?

This is a generalised list of suggestions, certainly not intended as either mandatory or exhaustive. The central point is that workers need to be in touch with their goals to aid effective work. Again revisiting such fundamentals might help the worker who has lost sight of appropriate boundaries and interventions, and facilitate exploration of the relevant issues.

Resources and planning

Having explored the goals that the supervisee sees as important to the client, themselves, and, where appropriate, the agency, it is now useful to initiate some investigation into what resources are required to enable those goals to be achieved. These might be of a personal or practical nature, or perhaps involve the expertise of other workers.

Brainstorming can be a useful technique here for getting in touch with resources. A brainstorm of resources for the worker finding difficulty with issues of sexual abuse and power may produce a list which includes:

- books;
- workers with expertise in the subject;
- training courses;

- personal counsellors;
- him- or herself;
- the client;
- the supervisor;
- significant personal friends and lovers;
- leisure activities;
- the dog;
- the pub;
- the swimming pool.

Planning for such a worker may include taking steps to read relevant material, a reminder to work closely with the client's agenda and not a personal agenda, to check personal stress levels, to seek a training course, to undertake some personal counselling and to give appropriate attention to personal relationships. The example is illustrative rather than exhaustive in order to make the point.

Such reflections may on occasion lead to the conclusion that the best interest of the client may be served by appropriate referral if the results of the counselling are not benefiting the client.

Training and information giving

At some point within the process of supervision, the supervisor may be called upon to venture an opinion or to offer ideas based upon his or her own professional experience and expertise. This point is optimally reached towards the end of supervision rather than at the beginning. In a spirit of empowerment, rather than inducing dependency, every opportunity is ideally given for the supervisee to develop individual insights and ideas.

However, it would be both wasteful and irresponsible for a supervisor to ignore obvious deficits in the supervisee's education or experience. Information giving, then, might be relevant when a counsellor encounters difficulties with sexual attraction. Disclosure may be appropriate that the counsellor is not alone in such difficulties, and the supervisee may need help or direction in identifying appropriate resources.

Information giving may be needed on the ethical stance. A supervisor may need to stipulate that if the supervisee continues with a particular technique or unethical practice, then 'X' will be the result. So that, for example, the worker who initiates or continues with a sexual relationship with the client must be told the consequences of such behaviour. Clear contracting at the beginning will have provided a context for such an eventuality, both if the behaviour is to be reported and if the contract cannot be continued.

Mutual contracting

The original contract may have specified the supervision required by the supervisee, but this may change as the supervisee develops. Training needs, timing, frequency or type of supervision may now be assessed more accurately. Thus a renegotiated contract for the next session appears to be the most appropriate point to complete the process.

Flexibility of the model

This model may be equally effectively employed in one-to-one, facilitated groups, peer group, or self-supervision. The advantage in any of these situations is that the purpose and logical sequence is not forgotten.

With one-to-one supervision, whatever the relationship of supervisor and supervisee, while it may not be absolutely necessary to hold an identical value orientation, it is against the interests of both supervisee and client group to have a supervisor who is unable to understand and embrace the concepts of a non-judgemental approach, genuineness and empathy. This view is coloured by experience, which falls in line on this occasion with Rogers' teachings (Rogers, 1961; Rogers and Stevens, 1967), relating supervision to the conditions of personal growth. At the very least, it must be agreed that good supervision cannot occur without the supervisee feeling safe to disclose the trickier aspects of his or her practice.

One of the greatest benefits of peer supervision or of group supervision (and the two might overlap) is the sharing of experiences, in terms of both personal and client-related issues. Dexter and Wash (1986) suggest that peer debrief is essential for well-being and personal efficiency. The argument can be extended to suggest that the client's best interest is served when everything possible is being done to ensure the worker's ability to practise safely and efficiently. An effective peer group might tackle issues from a casework presentation perspective, or from a theme perspective.

This latter approach may be particularly helpful for tackling the themes under review. While it might be difficult for individuals to have the courage to disclose a sexual attraction or an intervention which he or she suspects to be particularly exploitative, the group approach may foster shared recognition that these may be issues.

One person's disclosure of being attracted to a client, for example, may facilitate that of other members of the group. This can create a sense of safety and a relief that here is a shared issue. Such recognition is enormously enabling. When thought about, it is extremely unlikely that any worker will go through a whole career without ever feeling some level of sexual attraction to at least one client, or without some gratuitous pleasure resultant from the power of the relationship. Admittance of the range of human emotion can be immensely helpful, as can the sharing of strategies to combat difficulties.

Self-supervision involves a reflective approach, an ability to self-check and self-assess which enhances quality of work without inhibition through self-consciousness. This involves a degree of self-awareness, and an ability for self-analysis. Following a systematic approach can aid clarity here, in being able to achieve some distancing. Various aids may be appropriate, including tapes, notes and interpersonal process recall, an active reflective technique.

A worker who is sexually exploiting, or in danger of sexually exploiting, a client will know at some level that he or she is behaving in a way which is out of kilter with the general approach.[2] If the worker then self-supervises, the following types of questions will help in this reflection:

- How do I feel when I anticipate this client's arrival?
- How do I feel when the client arrives?
- How do I look at the client?
- What is my level of arousal?
- Where is my energy and enthusiasm – at what points do these manifest?
- Who directs the content of the sessions?
- How do I feel when the client leaves?
- How do I feel now as I reflect?
- Has the contract been maintained, or does it need renegotiation?

The answers may help achieve some clarity on what is happening in the counselling relationship.

Conclusions

The model described in this section is intended as being illustrative. Whatever approach is used, the point is that purposeful supervision can provide the forum for the worker's development and for the client's safety. It is accepted professional practice that counsellors

and psychotherapists do not work without supervision, and it may
be useful for prospective clients to explore with therapists what
supervisory provision they have for themselves. Ideally this information would be offered by the therapist. While supervision is only
as effective as the motivation of the counsellor and the skills of the
supervisor, it is an immensely valuable resource to ethically sound
practice.

Training

The training forum offers the potential for exploring the problems
and ethics of sexual boundaries through awareness raising, skills
training, enhanced understanding of interpersonal dynamics and the
modelling of good practice. Such modelling means that the
trainer(s) overtly set and maintain appropriate boundaries and thus
demonstrate a commitment to the relevant codes of ethics and
practice. This may act as a role model for how the trainee counsellor
would act in relation to clients.

At present, the possibility of therapist–client attraction is not
given close attention in most training. The one exception seems to
be within psychotherapy training where the concept of transference
is recognised and explored. Even here, there is little overt consideration of the realities of sexual attraction between therapist and
client, or of the possible desire to wield power. Some feminist
schools of training offer a more direct consideration of themes of
sexual politics, where it is recognised that there may be issues of
power imbalance between men and women.

Generally, however, the subject is notable by its absence. One
participant in this research puts the case forcefully that the possibility of therapist–client attraction must be seriously considered:

> If therapy is getting anywhere, you've got to have some of this
> [attraction] and if you've got a therapist who is charismatic and warm,
> you're going to have the psychosis of falling in love, and it's no different
> with a therapist than with anyone else, someone you meet in a bar
> somewhere, except the therapist has got vastly more power. . . . The
> only thing [the therapist] can do, is have regular supervision . . . and
> you've got to have your own therapy, because one day somebody is going
> to come along [who you're attracted to] . . . I suppose I just do not
> believe that there are good therapists who do not [sometimes] feel
> sexually attracted to their clients, they must do, it's human nature, and
> it's in the nature of therapy.

I agree totally that the probability of the therapist being attracted to
a client at some time must be recognised and therefore integrated

into therapy and counselling training. Themes of sexuality and power provide an important focus here, whatever the therapeutic model.

It is not appropriate to go through all the methods of training available to the therapeutic communities, but it is appropriate to offer a small selection of exercises which I and others have found useful. The strength in using them is that they offer the opportunity to examine the issues within a professional setting. Their use can be adapted to different therapeutic approaches. I include some amalgams of material generated to stimulate thought and to give the trainer some focus of what might need to be addressed.

In adding a word of caution, it is worth making the point that training at present depends on many idiosyncratic approaches, and there is a need for clearer models which systematically explore and link issues of exploitation and oppression within professional practice. In their absence, the caution is that these workshop formats are included on the understanding that they are useful as a method only where trainer and students are committed to the prospect of self-challenge within a learning climate which is conducive to this. They are not offered in order to name sexual exploitation as a 'topic' to be covered as the stereotypical tourist might 'do' France in a day! It is not my intention to suggest that if participants try these or similar exercises then they will have a . complete understanding of sex and sexism.

A framework is offered for each exercise, and there are some common conditions which need to be established for each. My own preference is to work with a co-trainer wherever possible for maximum benefit and safety for participants. It is understood that a clear contract is established with the group on the limits of confidentiality, timings, learning responsibility, and commitment to support and challenge. Safety in these conditions means that each participant is allowed to develop with respect while not being allowed to be cosily complacent. The presence of two trainers means that individual attention may be offered if participants become distressed.

Each exercise has a similar format. They only operate within a contracted setting; instructions are made as clearly as possible and time given for queries; responses are identified as emotional, cognitive or behavioural – what do you feel, what do you think, what do you do; and time is given for debrief. By this I mean the opportunity to raise any issues or share any responses that the student may need help with, the opportunity to express feelings about the exercise before leaving the room. Some training knowledge is assumed in giving this format, and the exercises are aimed at experienced trainers to use and adapt accordingly.

Responses to the situation

Aim: To raise awareness of the possibilities of client–counsellor or counsellor–client sexual attraction and to look at potential responses.

Resources needed: Large room, paper, pens, role-play scenario.

Method: In this exercise, a demonstration of a composite case is made to elicit reactions and responses. The idea is for two trainers to role-play a therapist–client situation wherein one or both parties feel a sexual attraction for the other. The role-play is pre-scripted and the trainers will have worked out already what kind of responses they will give to each other.

The training group is split into three groups and asked to observe the role-play from three perspectives – that of client, of counsellor, and of counsellor's supervisor. They are asked to observe with an eye to what feelings and thoughts are elicited for them, and to giving feedback on what interventions seem to be enabling or disabling.

The role-play is enacted for fifteen minutes. The three groups are then given five minutes to debrief immediate reactions, and the larger group is then drawn together to give feedback to the trainers and to discuss feelings, thoughts and perspectives. Timing depends on the size of the group, but it is important to give enough time for thorough discussion, and for acknowledgement of accompanying emotions. Trainers also need time for debriefing themselves out of role, and for debrief from any strong emotions that come their way during feedback. Like any work on sexual exploitation, the exercise may provoke powerful feelings.

Exercise overview: I have used this exercise with different gender dyads, and with client disclosing attraction or counsellor disclosing attraction. Many of the issues which arise have been common, with participants experiencing feelings of shock, disbelief, anxiety, confusion, frustration, the urge to deny, guilt, and anger. Some participants felt threatened and apprehensive that they would become impotent in such an event.

It is worth noting that a male colleague role-playing a rejecting counsellor provoked a great deal of anger in one group which was predominantly female. It can be useful in this situation to have feedback directed through the other trainer so that personal attack is discouraged.

Brainstorming possibilities

Aim: To raise awareness of how therapeutic workers might react or respond to hearing clients' sexual material, or to sexual attraction between them.

Resources needed: Large room, flipchart, pens, cue-cards for trainers.

Method: Split the training group into four and ask each subgroup to brainstorm what reactions are possible when they as workers are:

• aroused by the client's material;
• repelled by the client's material;
• attracted to the client;
• being propositioned by the client.

Many people are resistant to the idea that these really are possibilities, and then find brainstorming difficult to do. The trainer then needs to give some prompts which are ready on cue-cards. For example, the trainer might suggest that participants:

• Think of a favourite sexual fantasy, and then imagine being told it by a client.
• Imagine a scene of degradation that they have read or seen and then imagine a client telling them that as his or her experience.
• Think of someone who they find highly attractive walking through the door as their client.
• Recall scenes where they have been sexually propositioned and then imagine that this is happening within the counselling dyad.

The brainstorm format leaves it safe for individuals to share ideas without having to make personal disclosures. Participants may need help from the trainer in thinking as widely and ridiculously as possible, and to be reminded that they are not being asked to say how they *would* react, but to cover all eventualities of how they *might* react. These are then written down by the groups on flipchart paper. They may be divided into categories of feeling responses, thoughts and actions.

    Once brainstormed, groups are brought together to share their response sheets. Time needs to be allowed for debrief of participants' reactions to the elicited responses, as well as to how it felt actually doing the exercise.

Exercise overview: The following are a selection of responses which have been generated in my workshops, and may be helpful to the facilitator.

Turned on by material:
- Encourage the client to give more detail.
- Touch the client inappropriately.
- Meet outside the counselling forum – pub, home, bedroom.
- Suggest simulation, that is, work through this physically in the name of empathy.
- Terminate relationship.
- Stay with relationship and work through the issues.
- Seek supervision.
- Filter out or dismiss it.
- Oh shit!
- Is he (she) making it up because he (she) knows it's turning me on?
- I wonder if he (she) can tell I need to be careful?
- I wonder what would be *genuine* here.
- I should monitor my responses so that I don't stimulate similar feelings in the client.
- Change the subject.
- Feel angry – how dare you have control over me?

Turned off by material:
- Distance myself from the story.
- Feel afraid/guilty/voyeuristic.
- Feel fascinated.
- Feel numb/confused.
- Doubt the story, feel disbelief.
- Challenge the client about the reason for the material.
- Challenge myself about why I'm turned off.
- Feel responsiblity and collusion.
- Hot flush – shock, embarrassment.
- Feel scared/anxious.
- Feel angry.
- Feel admiration.
- Feel apologetic.
- Panic.
- Feel ignorant.

Attracted to client:
- Go to bed with the client.
- Make extra appointments.
- Flirt.

- Extra supervisions.
- Explain it as countertransference.
- Be honest about it.
- Denial that it's happening.
- Find out how the client feels.
- Blame/project onto client.
- Work with it.
- Refer on.
- Think in terms of client's history . . . and my own.
- Be aware of the dynamic.
- Collusion with the client's patterns.
- Kiss the client.
- Remove all clothing, my own, the client's, both.
- Watch a sex video.
- Rape.

Client attracted to counsellor:
- I thought I was past all this – supervision and don't pass go.
- I was never taught this on the course.
- Would you tell me some more about this?
- Help!
- Waste time and avoid the issue.
- Because we're two people there is likely to be a whole range of human emotion; feeling something is fine, acting on it is different.
- You're an attractive person, but I'm happily married (I think).
- How am I going to get out of this without really hurting the client?
- I must be a rotten counsellor.
- Start exploring issues around sexuality and authority.
- Tell the client you can't work with him or her.
- Thank you for sharing that with me; would you like to talk further about that?
- I'm (not) attracted to you.
- Waste time.
- Feel flattered, arrange more sessions.
- Feel threatened.
- Exploit the opportunity.

We may note that these lists can be subdivided into appropriate responses, curiosity responses, stunned responses, and, in places, humorous responses. Categorising these may be used as a second part to the exercise.

On occasion, participants have needed considerable challenge to be honest about the possible responses, and the importance of a safe learning climate becomes paramount. Initial reactions may need to be separated from those written down – how did it feel to consider these, to share them with someone else, to hear other people's responses? Do any of these remind us of how we have reacted in the past? It may be useful to look at which areas generated most or least appropriate responses, and which are most difficult.

Having identified what is easy and what is hard, it is helpful to take this further and identify the strengths that participants have. At the least these will include the motivation to explore the area and the courage to share apprehensions and difficulties. It is useful to work through to identifying further needs and how participants might get these met.

Gender assumptions

Aim: The aim of this exercise is to heighten awareness of the heterosexual assumptions we might make, and to develop some insight into how it feels to be part of a group which feels constrained by the community around them.

Resources needed: Large room, instruction cards.

Method: The group is split into two. Participants in one group are designated active listeners and those in the second group as clients. Active listeners are given the instruction to try to find out something about the client which will provide an idea of the client's current situation and any concerns or issues within it. The client group is given a brief card on which they are told the following: 'Talk about yourself and your immediate world without disclosing any information which identifies your sexual preference.'

The client's brief is then disclosed and the pairs discuss the experience themselves for ten minutes, noting what assumptions were made, what the cues were for such assumptions, whether it was difficult to keep something secret, etc. The group is then drawn together to share perspective.

Exercise overview: The person doing the active listening may or may not have made various assumptions, or might have noticed omissions. One response which I have encountered more than once, for example, is that women with children are assumed to be heterosexual.

The client may have found it difficult not to divulge information if unused to having to hide things. The client may also be angry if this is an alien experience. The exercise usually generates some stimulating discussion, and may provoke a range of feelings. Time needs to be calculated appropriately.

Awareness of personal sexual issues

Aim: The aim of this exercise is to raise participants' awareness of how easy or difficult it is to accept or share their own sexuality, and to relate this to how it might be for the client.

Resources needed: Large room, cushions, easy chairs.

Method: Participants are instructed to find a relaxing position and then taken through a standard relaxation exercise, tensing and relaxing the body and noting the rhythm of their breathing. They are then encouraged to try the following visualisation.

Imagine your sexual life as a chest of three drawers. What is the visual image that you get, how does it look, and how might it feel to touch. When you are ready, you are going to put those sexual feelings, experiences and thoughts that you find easy to accept and can share with anyone into the top drawer. Into the middle drawer go those thoughts, feelings and experiences which you would share with particular people, such as, friend or lover. Into the bottom drawer go those elements of your sexuality which are kept as undisclosable, and which may be private or secret. As you visualise the chest, you may choose to swap things around from drawer to drawer. What things are you swapping around, and what do they look like?

About fifteen minutes should be allowed for this exercise, and at the end participants are told to hold a visual image of the whole set of drawers and their contents, and to put away those they want to before completing the visualisation. This is important for those who have material which they find difficult. Participants are then allowed to return from their relaxed state into the room at a gentle pace. At the completion of the exercise, they are encouraged to share with one other person how the experience has felt for them.

The large group discussion will then take up any issues which individuals want to raise. It is useful for the trainer to make the connection between the experience of reflection for the participant and for the person in the client seat in counselling or therapy.

Exercise overview: For some participants this will hold no surprises, whereas others will get in touch with new insights which may be liberating or difficult. Again, debrief needs to be handled with sensitivity in a conducive climate. As with any visualisation exercise, the physical relaxation can induce a slightly hypnotic state, and I would not recommend this exercise for trainers who have not used visualisation before.

As well as stimulating self-awareness, I have found this useful as a means of reminding counsellors to hold clients' disclosures and issues in great respect and to acknowledge the trust invested in the process. It is no easier for a client to disclose than a counsellor, and this cannot be emphasised too often.

Sexual myths

Aim: The aim of this exercise is to explore some of the attitudes we hold about our own and others' sexuality, and to identify common myths.

Resources needed: Large room, flipcharts, paper, pens.

Method: Invite the group members to brainstorm any myths, any commonly held beliefs, that have had some impact on their sexuality or sexual development. One or two myths may be suggested to get the group going.

After brainstorming, invite individuals to rank the three out of the list which they feel has had most impact on their life. Invite them to discuss this with one other person. Open up large group discussion for developing any points which have been made, or for debriefing any personal issues.

Possible outcomes – some myths which the exercise has identified are detailed below:

- Girls are responsible, and mustn't let themselves go.
- Girls/women shouldn't 'lead a boy on'.
- You're asking to be raped – through dress, behaviour, etc.
- He can't help it – male sexuality is uncontrollable.
- Women are responsbible for heterosexual men's erections.
- Men *need* sex, women don't.
- Women must contrive sex for their male partners.
- Women are responsible for themselves, contraception and the consequences of sexual activity.
- Gay sex is abnormal, second best.
- Women are passive within sexual relationships.
- Active women are sluts, active men are studs, lads.
- *Real* sex is heterosexual, involves penetration and lots of orgasms, and ends with the man's ejaculation.
- Everyone else is having a whale of a time.
- It's not okay to be celibate – it's abnormal and a problem unless you're too old (because old people aren't sexual).
- Sex works with no communication.
- Sex is men's bit of fun – mainstream pornography is appropriate sexual stimulation sanctioned by various forces in society. It is not degrading in any way.

- Pornography is only used by straight men.
- Women shouldn't masturbate (and if they do they shouldn't tell).
- Women *should*/*must* have orgasms – vaginal, clitoral or g-spot??
- Prince/princess myth – men are rescuers, there to look after and take care of women.
- We have a completely free choice.
- Women never abuse.

Exercise overview: Such myths are powerful and can have deep impact on sexual attitude and behaviour. They are one way in which the social construction of sexuality is made and maintained. Facilitators of this exercise need to leave plenty of time for debrief and discussion. Some people may feel strongly about the issues raised. There may not be consensus between whether statements are mythical or not. Again, the debrief needs to be handled with sensitivity.

Values

I have suggested elsewhere that all counsellors take their own value system into the therapeutic encounter, however much they might suspend judgement. It can be useful to point up what those are for each individual. One method of doing this is to tie them into ethical stances. The following approach may be useful.

Aim: To raise awareness of participants' value systems and what dilemmas they may feel.

Resources needed: Large room, flip chart, paper, pens.

Method: The group is split into subgroups of four and each offered a different scenario to work at in the style of 'what would you do in this situation?' I would suggest that the actual scenarios may be tailored to the particular group. For example school nurses who use counselling skills may profit from exploration of different issues from counsellors in a genito-urinary medicine clinic, or psycho-dynamic therapists. Some possible scenarios may be:

- What would you do if a client discloses underage sexual activity? Does it make any difference if a pregnancy is involved, or if the client admits sexual behaviour which may put him- or herself or others at risk?
- How do you react if a client discloses that he or she is sexually abusing someone else? What factors would influence your decision?

- What do you do if you know that a colleague is exploiting a client for personal sexual gratification? Does it make any difference if the client involved assures you that this is all right?
- What would you do if you know that a client who is HIV+ is having unprotected sex with someone you know, without having disclosed his or her status:

Having considered the scenarios, the large group reforms to explore the issues, the points of conflict, and the resources they may have around them to help deal with such situations.

Exercise overview: Such scenarios help to get in touch with what *feelings* the situations provoke, what *thoughts* the counsellor might be left with, and what *action*, if any, the counsellor might like to take. The major issues seem to be about confidentiality, responsibility, dependency and conflict between personal and agency ethics. It is my experience that many workers operate in something of a vacuum until they find themselves in a situation which provokes dilemmas. The clearer we can be about personal and agency boundaries from the outset, the clearer the service for the client.

In debriefing the exercise, it is important to acknowledge the feelings which might arise. It is common for difficulties and differences between points of view to be identified. It is then helpful to raise awareness of strengths and resources to complete the exercise – 'What have you done in the past that works well?', 'Who might be helpful to you if faced with this situation?', 'What would make your position (and the client's) clearer here?' Often the right of supervision and the importance of clear contracting emerge at this point.

Conclusions

These exercises give a basis from which to develop training sessions which focus on areas of sexuality. Trainers will obviously use their own experience and expertise to tap the relevant issues. Before leaving this section, it is relevant to remind therapists of all kinds that training is not a one-off event, it is perhaps something to be ongoing. Moreover, trainers also need support. It would be useful to see support and development groups which explore issues as well as skills and dilemmas, as well as more clear cut themes. Some initiatives do exist but more are needed. Any ongoing work which recognises that therapy is a skilled job which entails responsibility would be helpful.

Finally, there is a need for trainers and therapists to revisit the skills of listening and responding. This may seem obvious, but one of the repeated failings where therapy becomes exploitative is that of not imparting clarity. Clear communication skills which aid the client's understanding of what is going on are central to the job, and often lacking among even the most experienced. These skills make for the foundation of ethical practice.

Notes

1   It is commonly recognised among professionals and survivors that childhood sexual abuse may be conceptualised as a loss – loss of childhood, ego identity, security, trust, etc.

2   This comment is necessarily generalised, but will hold true for all but those who deliberately set out to exploit every client. Even multiple offenders usually have some clients whom they do not exploit in the same way, and so self-supervision will highlight the differences. The obvious limitation is that the multiple or intentional offender may be one who will deliberately not reflect on the ethical standard of his or her practice.

9

CONCLUSIONS AND RECOMMENDATIONS

Several areas have been considered and it seems helpful to sub-divide them as follows; restating the problem, self-exploration, education, training, supervision, contracting, awareness raising for clients, reparatory work, and further research exploration. This is not an exhaustive list, and some areas invariably overlap, but my intention is to make some suggestions and hopefully to stimulate further discussion. This is a self-referential chapter, in the sense of offering some contribution to the educative process which it advocates. In the spirit of enquiry in which this work has been pursued, theory and practice are integrated through ideas and examples.

Restating the problem

It seems clear that within the practice of therapy, there is the potential for sexually exploitative behaviour on the part of the therapist. This potential is abused by some practitioners. It can take many forms, ranging from the display of attitudes through non-verbal behaviour to overt sexual assault. Sometimes it seems to demonstrate unmitigated intent, whereas at the other end of the scale it may suggest an unwitting causing of offence through ignorance, lack of skill or lack of awareness.

It seems equally clear that the effect of exploitative behaviour is manifold. For some clients it causes confusion and suspicion and for others a much more severe damage. It is often experienced as one in a series of exploitations and will be interpreted within the client's experiential history. For example, it may have different effects if a client has been previously sexually abused or not. At its worst, it seems that such behaviour is felt to be the catalyst for suicidal behaviour, where the client, in a particularly vulnerable state, feels exploited and devalued by their last source of help.

It does not seem particularly helpful to attribute blame and advocate punishment for the therapists concerned without consideration of the wider context. At the same time it is essential that exploitative behaviour is seen as their responsibility and that the professions concerned state this publicly. It is never the fault or the responsibility of the client. Moreover, professionals need to be honest and admit that there is some collusion with exploitative practice within the therapeutic professions, whether this is intentional or not. This is demonstrated on a scale of sexist practice and attitude which ranges from inappropriate comments or material to overt covering up and collusion with offending practitioners.

A further difficulty to date has been a lack of awareness in the professions involved. It seems that many therapists do not realise that the problem even exists. This is not helped when the possibilities of either sexual attraction, or of the potential for abuse, are not adequately addressed in training, if at all. There is ignorance about the effect of such exploitation on the clients involved and about how to work reparatively with abused clients.

For the exploited parties, there is little easily accessible help available. It can be difficult to realise that such exploitation is not their fault, and then to find a trusted party in whom they can confide. There are then obstacles to be negotiated in trying to either get help or to make a complaint in a supported and helpful way. Often the complaints procedures are either inadequate, mistrusted, or simply unknown.

It is therefore encumbent upon the professions concerned to see this problem as one to be both owned and addressed by them. While my personal philosophy sees punishment as an unhelpful strategy, I would argue that we have a responsibility to ensure as far as possible that offending practitioners do not continue sanctioned practice. Further, we must undertake to do as much as possible towards preventive practice, to engender a forum for practitioners to declare uncertainties and dilemmas, to raise awareness of the problem and to introduce what strategies we can. This is likely to entail a commitment to adopting a perspective which is both intra- and interorganisational, and which reflects a moral stance where the first responsibility is to the client.

We can target various strategic areas as some means to this end. Some overlap and yet may be seen as being discrete from each other.

Awareness raising through literature

The intention of this book is to be educative, and the higher the profile of education in this area, the better. Two recent additions to the literature are by Brian Thorne (1991) and Peter Thomas (1991). Brian Thorne writes about his erotic contact with a client which he claims as a sort of ultimate client-centred therapy. Peter Thomas talks about his struggle with feeling sexually attracted to a client, a struggle which he takes to supervision, thus enabling him to continue the counselling without acting on the attraction.

Whatever we think about the two strategies expounded, and I have to say that my preference is strongly for the second, it seems to me that the more public discussion about the issue, the higher the awareness raising. This might provide a more open climate for counsellor self-exploration. The danger of course is that it simply becomes a forum for a sort of 'true confessions', which would be not only unproductive but damaging. While this danger must be acknowledged, it still seems better to have real possibilities recognised rather than denied.

Supervision

Regular and thorough supervision seems to be an essence of good practice. The process is at its best when it is as clear and methodical as possible, and to that end my preference is to use a systematic client-centred model of supervision which has been developed with a colleague. This is represented in Chapter 8.

There is increasing interest in supervision in the therapeutic professions, and an increasing amount of literature is available. The points I particularly want to reiterate here are, that supervision is a necessity to good practice rather than a luxury, that it needs to be enabling rather than constricting, that it is a skilled process, and that it is *for the client's interests and safety*. Good supervision is one way to pre-empt an overstepping of boundaries.

Complaints procedures and ethics committees

One of the points which has been made is that ethics committees are difficult to approach for a number of reasons. Because of the difficulties, many clients never get as far as making a complaint. Perhaps if we want this path to be open to clients, we need to go back a step and learn from the reactions which we have before us.

One participant made the point strongly.

I rang [the organisation] and the person who answered the phone in the

office said well, we have got a complaints procedure and we will send you
a copy of it. And then she said if you put your complaint in writing, it will
be highly confidential. . . . I said I would like to talk to somebody about
whether I should need to make a complaint, or what would happen. . . .
OK, the complaints procedure tells you, it's all written out, but it's too
far, for a subject as difficult as abuse within that relationship. You can't
get from where you are at to make a written statement and send it to
some impersonal organisation you've never come across. . . . There has
got to be some friendly body at the end of the phone somewhere and you
can make an arrangement to meet at a certain time and then discuss
whether you should be making a complaint and you could be validated
and then feel you can go ahead. . . . Whoever I spoke to sounded like an
admin. person who said oh, it's all confidential and I don't deal with
interviews and no one can speak to you, you will just have to send us a
written complaint.

So, although it seems ironic that it should be the case in an area so
concerned with quality of communication, we need to remember
that the first point of contact should be user-friendly – responses
need to be clear and empathic, and to offer information which lets
users know what their possibilities are.

One thing that strikes me as being a useful second point would be
to have designated consultants available on a nationwide basis who
might be the first port of call to meet with. I was very conscious
when I conducted this research of how relieved some participants
were to be able to talk through their experience with someone who
believed them without trying to counsel or advise. It seems to me
that there is a real need here for the sort of service where people
could do this, find out what the procedure would entail, and then
perhaps make the next decision.

Talking with professionals may not be the only need. It might be a
useful strategy if trying to work out whether or not to make a
complaint with any particular organisation. Exploited parties often
want to talk to others with similar experiences. There are growing
networks for people who feel that they have been exploited in
therapy. Organisations need to be much more aware of who these
are. At the very least, appropriate telephone numbers need to be
known and given out to enquirers. Perhaps in the long term there
might be much more real communication between networks and
professionals.

If clients were able to be confident that their first enquiry would
be dealt with appropriately and that they could be supported in
taking the decision whether or not to complain, the third step would
be to make the complaints system more accessible, and to be seen to
be fair. One of the concerns referred to earlier in this book is that

ethics committees may be 'contaminated', or may be perceived as being contaminated.

There are several strategies available to diffuse anxieties and to check out whether they are founded or not. I say this from a perspective where I have no doubt that there are some heavily biased and prejudicial committees in operation. I am also aware that there are people within organisations who would like to see this changed.

One first step needs to be that professional organisations have publicly available details of who their ethics committees are made up of, with relevant biographical details. At the very least, this lets users know if people who they *do not* want to approach are on the relevant panels. It seems important for the purpose of facilitating trust that as much mystery and unknown elements be eliminated as possible.

Secondly, it seems crucial and logical that there should be some system of arbitration within ethical committees. However well-intentioned particular individuals or groups are, while organisations are purely self-disciplinary they will carry their blind spots. My preference would be that clients who complain are allowed someone of their choosing to be with them to offer support where necessary, and that at least one independent arbitrator be involved in any complaint procedure. I have no doubt that this would provoke conflicting responses and that there may be difficulties mechanically, but this issue needs serious attention. What needs to be looked at is mechanisms for making the process meaningful and fair for the client.

Whatever is done, my guess is that it will remain difficult for people to either have complete faith in ethics committees or to be able to use them. One participant voices this strongly. I had asked if there was any mechanism that the participant would like to see in place which would help clients ask for help or make a complaint:

> I don't think there's any way . . . I don't think it's a problem that any patient or client should ever have to deal with. I just don't think you're in the right place . . . I mean, I remember the day I went to see her . . . it was total love . . . the psychotic feeling that you get when you fall in love – love is a psychotic state and I think therefore you are dealing with mechanisms for which precisely the patient cannot be held to be responsible . . . so I don't believe there's anything the patient can honestly do.

In this scenario, then, the client is so besotted that he or she cannot even see anything wrong, let alone be expected to act with responsibility. As the process becomes recognised as exploitative, presumably this perspective is replaced with one which is heavily influenced by self-doubt. In the words of one of the participants:

I thought they'd think, oh God, another hysterical woman.

There is an irony in this particular participant being a therapist herself – if this is how we perceive the structures, what of those completely unfamiliar with them? While not wishing to see clients as helpless individuals, I think that there is much sense in this – not only should it not be the responsibility of the client to make all the initiatives, sometimes it cannot be.

Issues of reporting

Much more attention needs to be given to the issues of therapists reporting others whom they know to be abusing clients. In the first place, they need to know to whom they can go, and in what circumstances, for discussion. Often they may be facing dilemmas, particularly where some confidentiality may need to be broken. They then might need to know what format is in place should they decide to report. They need to know to whom to report, and whether or not to confront the other professional first. It could be that codes of ethics and practice need to state more fully that it is unethical to sanction or to collude with exploitative practice.

It is not appropriate to offer any kind of blueprint here, suffice it to say that more attention needs to be given to this matter. Any strategy which enables practitioners to break the wall of silence and to deconstruct collusive practice needs to be considered seriously.

Client-support groups

Since the late 1980s, several people have taken initiatives to try to seek, give or share support for those who find themselves exploited. There are now networks in the United Kingdom. The major ones of which I am aware are the following.

Abuse in Therapy Support Network
c/o Women's Support Project
871 Springfield Road
Glasgow G31 4HZ
The main aim of this organisation is to offer support and infor-

mation to people who have felt abused in therapy. It operates within a feminist context concerned to address issues relating to male violence. The organisation does not offer counselling but can suggest appropriate sources for those who wish to have counselling.

The Prevention of Professional Abuse Network (POPAN) was set up to address the issue of sexual abuse in psychotherapy. It concentrates on the damage to the abused persons, their stories and subsequent events. Monthly support meetings are held. The organisation is interested to hear from interested parties, including therapists who have abused, to try to develop a clearer overview. They may be contacted at:
Flat 1, 20 Daleham Gardens
London NW3 5DA

Neither the Abuse in Therapy Support Network, nor POPAN, receives funding and stamped addressed envelopes with enquiries are appreciated.

The purpose of the groups is manifold. The primary focus is on helping the abused individual.

Clients charters

It would be useful for clients to be as informed as possible before entering any contract of therapy what they should *not* expect within it. Various client groups have come up with suggestions and advice as to what factors to take into consideration when choosing a therapist, and clarity over what boundaries clients might expect to be kept. There may well be benefits in user groups and professionals working together to produce a charter which is available to clients.

Conclusions

The areas outlined in this chapter are just some of those which need to be explored in much more depth. Hopefully they will stimulate the reader to think of others and to begin addressing them. I am very much aware that there is no blueprint for stopping exploitation, and that we operate in a value-laden society where the practice of therapy is both influenced and influential. At best, perhaps, we can improve the quality of practice and demystify some of the processes involved in the hope that this empowers rather than disables the client.

I remain optimistic, however, that there is value in exposing exploitation, and in the exploited being able to be heard and helped in appropriate ways. It seems to me that exploitation in the name of therapy is against all our interests and should not be hidden away as a secret unnamed problem.

REFERENCES

Adams, C.D. (1987) 'Sex with patients: is it malpractice?', *Trial*, 23: 58–61.

Association of Sexual and Marital Therapists (1986) *Code of Ethics*. Sheffield: ASMT.

Austin, K., Moline, M. and Williams, G.T. (1990) *Confronting Malpractice: Legal and Ethical Dilemmas in Psychotherapy*. Newbury Park: Sage.

Bannister, D. and Fransella, F. (1986) (3rd Edn) *Inquiring Man: The Psychology of Personal Constructs*. London: Routledge.

Barnhouse, R. (1978) 'Sex between patient and therapist', *Journal of the American Academy of Psychoanalysis* 6(4): 533–46.

Bohart, A.C. and Todd, J. (1988) *Foundations of Clinical and Counselling Psychology*. New York: Harper Row.

Bouhoutsos, J. (1985) 'Therapist–client sexual involvement: a challenge for mental health professionals and educators', *American Journal of Orthopsychiatry*, 55(2): 177–82.

Boyd, J. (1978) *Counselor Supervision: Approaches Preparation Practices*. Indiana: Accelerated Development.

British Association for Counselling (1984) *Code of Ethics and Practice for Counsellors*. Rugby: BAC.

British Association for Counselling (1985) *Code of Ethics and Practice for Counsellors*. Rugby: BAC.

British Association for Counselling (1990) *Code of Ethics and Practice for Counsellors*. Rugby: BAC.

British Psychological Society (1985) 'A code of conduct for psychologists', *Bulletin of the British Psychological Society*.

Broverman, I.K., Broverman, D. and Clarkson, F.E. (1970) 'Sex-role stereotypes and clinical judgements of mental health', *Journal of Consulting and Clinical Psychology*, 34(1): 1–7.

Chertok, L. and de Saussure, R. (1979) Trans. by R.H. Ahrenfeldt. *The Therapeutic Revolution; from Mesmer to Freud*. New York: Brunner, Mazel.

Chesler, P. (1971) 'Patient and patriarch: women in the therapeutic relationship', in V. Gornick and B. Moran (eds), *Women in Sexist Society: Studies in Power and Powerlessness*. New York: Basic Books.

Cole, M. and Dryden, W. (1988) *Sex Therapy in Britain*. Milton Keynes: OU Press.

Coleman, E. and Schaefer, S. (1986) 'Boundaries of sex and intimacy between client and counsellor', *Journal of Counselling and Development*, 64: 341–4.

Comfort, A. (1974) *The Joy of Sex: Gourmet Guide to Lovemaking*. London: Quartet Books.

Comfort, A. (1977) *More Joy of Sex*. London: Quartet Books.

Cooper, G. (1988) 'Pregnancy counselling'. Training paper for British Pregnancy Advisory Service. First published in *Counselling News* (July 1980).

Davidson, V. (1977) 'Psychiatry's problem with no name: therapist–patient sex', *American Journal of Psychoanalysis*, 37: 43–50.

Davis, J. (1989) 'Issues in the evaluation of counsellors by supervisors', *Counselling*, 69 (Aug): 31–7.

Derosis, H., Hamilton, J., Morrison, E. and Strauss, M. (1987) Letter to *American Journal of Psychiatry* 144:5.

Dexter, G. and Russell, J. (1991) 'A client-centred model of supervision', in *The Egan Summer School Handbook*. York: University College of Ripon & York St John.

Dexter, G. and Wash, M. (1986) *Psychiatric Nursing Skills: A patient-centred approach*. Beckenham: Croom Helm.

Durre, L. (1980) 'Comparing romantic and therapeutic relationships', in K. Pope, (ed.), *On Love and Loving: Psychological Perspectives on the Nature and Experience of Romantic Love*. San Francisco: Jossey–Bass.

Egan, G. (1973) *Face to Face: The Small-Group Experience and Interpersonal Growth*. California: Brooks/Cole.

Egan, G. (1990) (4th Edn) *The Skilled Helper: A Systematic Approach to Effective Helping*. California: Brooks/Cole.

Ellis, A. and Whiteley, J.M. (1979) *Theoretical and Empirical Foundations of Rational-Emotive Therapy*. California: Brooks/Cole.

Foucault, M. (1977) *Discipline and Punish*. Harmondsworth: Penguin.

Foucault, M. (1981) *The History of Sexuality. Vol. 1*. Harmondsworth: Penguin.

Foucault, M. (1985) *Madness and Civilization*. London: Tavistock Publications.

Fransella, F. and Dalton, P. (1990) *Personal-Construct Counselling in Action*. London: Sage.

Freud, S. (1905) 'Three Essays on the Theory of Sexuality', pp. 125–243 in *The Standard Edition of the Complete Psychological Works of Sigmund Freud* (1953–74, Vol.7). London: Hogarth.

Friedan, B. (1965) *The Feminine Mystique*. London: Penguin.

Fromm, E. (1974) *The Art of Loving*. New York: Harper & Row.

Garrett, T. (1992) *Survey of sexually intimate behaviour with clients among clinical psychologists*. Unpublished MSc dissertation, University of Warwick.

Gartrell, N., Herman, J., Olarte, S., Feldstein, M., and Localio, J. (1986) 'Psychiatrist–patient sexual contact: results of a national survey, I: Prevalence', *American Journal of Psychiatry*, 143(9): 1126–31.

Gartrell, N., Herman, J., Olarte, S., Feldstein, M., and Localio, R. (1987) 'Reporting practices of psychiatrists who knew of sexual misconduct by colleagues', *American Journal of Orthopsychiatry*, 57(2): 267–95.

Gestalt Psychotherapy Training Institute (UK) (1988) *Draft Code of Ethics*.

HMSO (1983) *Mental Health Act*. London: HMSO.

Hart, J. (1979) *Social Work and Sexual Conduct*. London: Routledge & Kegan Paul.

Hays, J. Ray. (1980) 'Sexual contact between psychotherapist and patient: legal remedies', *Psychological Reports*, 47: 1247–54.

Heath, S. (1982) *The Sexual Fix*. London: Macmillan Press.

Herman, J., Gartrell, N., Olarte, S., Feldstein, M. and Localio, R. (1987) 'Psychiatrist–patient sexual contact: results of a national survey, II: Psychiatrists' Attitudes', *American Journal of Psychiatry*, 144(2): 164–9.

Hite, S. (1977) *The Hite Report*. Hamlyn: Summit.

Holroyd, J. and Bouhoutsos, J. (1985) 'Biased reporting of therapist–patient sexual intimacy', *Professional Psychology – Research and Practice*, 16(5): 701–9.

Holroyd, J. and Brodsky, A. (1977) 'Psychologists' attitudes and practices regarding erotic and nonerotic physical contact with patients', *American Psychologist*, 32: 843–9.

Institute of Humanistic and Traditional Psychotherapies (1989) *Ethical Standards*.

Institute of Psychotherapy and Social Studies (1989) *Ethical Principles and Practice* (5th draft). London: IPSS.

Karasu, T.B. (1980) 'The ethics of psychotherapy', *American Journal of Psychiatry* 137(12): 1502–12.

Kardener, S., Fuller, M. and Mensh, I. (1973) 'A survey of physicians' attitudes and practices regarding erotic and non-erotic contact with patients', *American Journal of Psychiatry*, 130(10): 1077–81.

Kinsey, A. (1948) *Sexual Behavior in the Human Male*. Philadelphia: W.B. Saunders.

Kinsey, A. (1953) *Sexual Behavior in the Human Female*. Philadelphia: W.B. Saunders.

Lange, J. and Hirsh, H. (1981) 'Legal problems of intimate therapy', *Medical Trial Technique*, 28(2): 201–8.

Lee, N. (1969) *The Search for an Abortionist*. Chicago: University of Chicago Press.

Leesfield, I. (1987) 'Negligence of mental health professionals: what conduct breaches standards of care', *Trial*, March: 57–61.

Marmor, J. (1972) 'Sexual acting out in psychotherapy', *American Journal of Psychoanalysis*, 32(1): 3–8.

Martin, J.P. (1984) *Hospitals in Trouble*. Oxford: Blackwell.

Maslow, A.H. (1970) revd edn. *Motivation and Personality*. New York: Harper & Row.

Masson, J. (1984) *The Assault on Truth: Freud's Suppression of the Seduction Theory*. London: Faber & Faber.

Masson, J. (1988) *Against Therapy*. London: Fontana.

Masters, W. and Johnson, V. (1970) *Human Sexual Inadequacy*. London: Churchill.

Morrow, C. (1987) 'Commentary: sex in the MD's office', *Hastings Center Report*, p. 12.

Munro, E., Manthei, R. and Small, J. (1983) *Counselling: A Skills Approach*. New Zealand: Methuen.

National Register of Hypnotherapists and Psychotherapists (1989) *Code of Ethics*. Nelson: NRHP.

Nelson-Jones, R. (1982) *The Theory and Practice of Counselling Psychology*. London: Holt.

Plummer, K. (1975) *Sexual Stigma: An Interactionist Account*. London: Routledge & Kegan Paul.

Pope, K. (1986) 'Research and laws regarding therapist–patient sexual involvement: implications for therapists', *American Journal of Psychotherapy*, 40(4): 564–71.

Pope, K. (1987) 'Preventing therapist–patient sexual intimacy: therapy for a therapist at risk', *Professional Psychology: Research and Practice*, 18(6): 624–8.

Pope, K. (1989) 'Therapist–patient sex syndrome: a guide for attorneys and subsequent therapists to assessing damage', in G. Gabbard (ed.) *Sexual Exploitation in Professional Relationships*. Washington, DC: American Psychiatric Press.

Pope, K. and Bouhoutsos, J. (1986) *Sexual Intimacy Between Therapists and Patients*. New York: Praeger.

Rapp, M.S. (1987) 'Sexual Misconduct', *Canadian Medical Association Journal*, 173(3): 193–4.

Rock, P. (1973) *Deviant Behaviour*. London: Hutchinson.
Rogers, C.R. (1951) *Client-Centred Therapy: Its Current Practice, Implications and Theory*. London: Constable.
Rogers, C.R. (1961) *On Becoming a Person: A Therapist's View of Psychotherapy*. London: Constable.
Rogers, C.R. (1978) *Carl Rogers On Personal Power: Inner Strength and Its Revolutionary Impact*. London: Constable.
Rogers, C.R. and Stevens, B. (1967) *Person to Person: The Problem of Being Human*. London: Souvenir Press.
Rose, N. (1990) *Governing the Soul: The Shaping of the Private Self*. London: Routledge.
Russell, J. (1990) 'Breaking boundaries: a research note', in *Counselling*, May: 47–50.
Rutter, P. (1990) *Sex in the Forbidden Zone*. London: Mandala.
Shapiro, E. (1987) 'Commentary: sex in the MD's office', *Hastings Center Report*, June 11–12.
Shepard, M. (1976) *Fritz*. New York: Bantam Books.
Smith, J.T. (1988) 'Therapist–patient sex: exploitation of the therapeutic process', *Psychiatric Annals*, 18(1): 59–63.
Sonne, J., Meyer, C.B. and Borys, D. (1985) 'Clients' reactions to sexual intimacy in therapy', *American Journal of Orthopsychiatry*, 55(2): 183–9.
Stanton, M. (1990) *Sandor Ferenczi: Reconsidering Active Intervention*. London: Free Association Books.
Szasz, T. (1971) *The Manufacture of Madness: A Comparative Study of the Inquisition and the Mental Health Movement*. London: Routledge & Kegan Paul.
Thomas, K. (1971) *Religion and the Decline of Magic*. Harmondsworth: Penguin.
Thomas, P. (1991) 'A therapeutic journey through the Garden of Eden', *Counselling*, 2(4): 143–5.
Thorne, B. (1991) *Person-Centred Counselling: Therapeutic and Spiritual Dimensions*. London: Whurr.
Tschudin, V. (1987) *Counselling Skills for Nurses*. (2nd Edn). London: Balliere Tindall.
Urbano, J. (1984) 'Supervision of counsellors: ingredients for effectiveness', *Counselling*, Nov.: 7–15.
Vance, C. and Snitow, A. (1984) *Pleasure and Danger: Exploring Female Sexuality*. London: Routledge & Kegan Paul.
Weber, M. (1968a) *Economy and Society: Vol. I*, G. Roth and C. Wittich (eds). Berkeley: University of California.
Weber, M. (1968b) *Economy and Society: Vol. II*, G. Roth and C. Wittich (eds). Berkeley: University of California.
Weeks, J. (1986) *Sexuality*. London: Ellis Horwood.

INDEX